University of San Francisco
San Francisco, California

Written by Sara Allshouse
Edited by Jessica Pecsenye, Justine Ezarik

Additional contributions by Omid Gohari,
Christina Koshzow, Chris Mason, Adam burns, Joey Rahimi,
Jon Skindzier, Luke Skurman, Tim Williams, Alan Evankovich,
and Kimberly Moore

ISBN # 1-59658-180-8
ISSN# 1552-1745

Special thanks to Babs Carryer, Andy Hannah, LaunchCyte, Tim O'Brien, Bob Sehlinger, Thomas Emerson, Andrew Skurman, Barbara Skurman, Bert Mann, Dave Lehman, Daniel Fayock, Chris Babyak,The Donald H. Jones Center for Entrepreneurship, Terry Slease, Jerry McGinnis, Bill Ecenberger, Idie McGinty, Kyle Russell, Jacque Zaremba, Larry Winderbaum, Paul Kelly, Roland Allen, Jon Reider, Team Evankovich, Julie Fenstermaker, Lauren Varacalli, Abu Noaman, Jason Putorti, Mark Exler, Daniel Steinmeyer, Jared Cohon, Gabriela Oates., Glen Meakem and David Koegler.

Extra Special thanks to Sandy Teixera, Freddie Wiant, J.P. Manuel and Anne MArie Nowak.

Bounce Back Team: Dave Rinehart, Viola Lasmana and Aaron Olivas.

College Prowler™
5001 Baum Blvd.
Suite 456
Pittsburgh, PA 15213

Phone: (412) 697-1390, 1(800) 290-2682
Fax: (412) 697-1396, 1(800) 772-4972
E-mail: info@collegeprowler.com
Website: www.collegeprowler.com

Welcome to College Prowler™

During the writing of College Prowler's guidebooks, we felt it was critical that our content was unbiased and unaffiliated with any college or university. We think it's important that our readers get honest information and a realistic impression of the student opinions on any campus — that's why if any aspect of a particular school is terrible, we (unlike a campus brochure) intend to publish it. While we do keep an eye out for the occasional extremist — the cheerleader or the cynic — we take pride in letting the students tell it like it is. We strive to create a book that's as representative as possible of each particular campus. Our books cover both the good and the bad, and whether the survey responses point to recurring trends or a variation in opinion, these sentiments are directly and proportionally expressed through our guides.

College Prowler guidebooks are in the hands of students throughout the entire process of their creation. Because you can't make student-written guides without the students, we have students at each campus who help write, randomly survey their peers, edit, layout, and perform accuracy checks on every book that we publish. From the very beginning, student writers gather the most up-to-date stats, facts, and inside information on their colleges. They fill each section with student quotes and summarize the findings in editorial reviews. In addition, each school receives a collection of letter grades (A through F) that reflect student opinion and help to represent contentment, prominence, or satisfaction for each of our 20 specific categories. Just as in grade school, the higher the mark the more content, more prominent, or more satisfied the students are with the particular category.

Once a book is written, additional students serve as editors and check for accuracy even more extensively. Our bounce-back team — a group of randomly selected students who have no involvement with the project — are asked to read over the material in order to help ensure that the book accurately expresses every aspect of the university and its students. This same process is applied to the 200-plus schools College Prowler currently covers. Each book is the result of endless student contributions, hundreds of pages of research and writing, and countless hours of hard work. All of this has led to the creation of a student information network that stretches across the nation to every school that we cover. It's no easy accomplishment, but it's the reason that our guides are such a great resource.

When reading our books and looking at our grades, keep in mind that every college is different and that the students who make up each school are not uniform — as a result, it is important to assess schools on a case-by-case basis. Because it's impossible to summarize an entire school with a single number or description, each book provides a dialogue, not a decision, that's made up of 20 different topics and hundreds of student quotes. In the end, we hope that this guide will serve as a valuable tool in your college selection process. Enjoy!

OMID GOHARI ○ CHRISTINA KOSHZOW ○ CHRIS MASON ○ JOEY RAHIMI ○ LUKE SKURMAN ○
The College Prowler™ Team

Table of Contents

Introduction from the Author

When people think of the University of San Francisco, odds are that they are just thinking of San Francisco. In fact, the majority of students who research the school just happen to come across it when searching for universities in San Francisco. But USF is more than a school that just happens to be in the right place at the right time. Besides being a prestigious Jesuit Catholic university with impeccable standards, the University of San Francisco values itself on attracting intellectual, diverse, and ethically strong individuals.

Currently, the University faces a time of tremendous growth; this year's freshmen class alone broke the record for the largest enrolled class in USF history. Because of the popularity of the school and of living in a city like San Francisco, problems are constantly arising around the need for more space, accommodations, and quality. The University of San Francisco is conscious of these needs and has been making every effort to solve them. At this very moment, USF is adding an entirely new building to the campus and in addition to renovating some of the older ones. Also, since I transferred here three years ago, USF has implemented countless renovations and additions, including the brand-new Loyola Village apartment-style residence hall.

As far as I'm concerned, anyone new to the University of San Francisco couldn't have come at a better time. The facilities are vastly improving, the faculty is always top-notch, and the diversity of the school-one of its most charming aspects-is at an all-time high. Aside from these perks, I hope that by reading this book, you will find that students here are enthusiastic about their education and truly enjoy life at USF. Most importantly, the University of San Francisco and the city of San Francisco make an outstanding combination sure to give you the most rewarding and exciting college experience.

Sara Allshouse, Author
University of San Francisco

By the Numbers

General Information

University of San Francisco
2130 Fulton Street
San Francisco, CA 94117

Control:
Private

Academic Calendar:
Semester

Religious Affiliation:
Jesuit Catholic

Founded:
1855

Website:
http://www.usfca.edu

Main Phone:
(415) 422-5555

Admissions Phone:
(415) 422-6563

Student Body

**Full-Time
Undergraduates:**
4,493

**Part-Time
Undergraduates:**
225

**Total Male
Undergraduates:**
1,668

**Total Female
Undergraduates:**
3,050

Female: Male Ratio:
64.6% : 35.4%

Admissions

Overall Acceptance Rate:
82%

Early Action Acceptance Rate:
72%

Regular Acceptance Rate:
85.0%

Total Applicants:
4,634

Total Acceptances:
3,798

Freshman Enrollment:
321

Yield (% of admitted students who actually enroll):
24.2%

Early Action Available?
Yes

Transfer Applications Recieved:
998

Transfer Applicants Offered Admission:
800

Transfer Students Enrolled:
359

Transfer Applications Acceptance Rate:
80%

Regular Decision Deadline:
February 1

Regular Decision Notification:
March 1

Early Action Deadline:
November 15

Early Action Notification:
End of December

Must-Reply-By Date:
May 1

Common Application Accepted?
Yes

Supplemental Forms?
Yes

Admissions Phone:
1-800-CALL-USF

Admissions E-mail:
academics@usfca.edu

Admissions Website:
http://www.usfca.edu/acadserv/adm ission/index.html

SAT I or ACT Required?
Either.

First-Year Students Submitting SAT Scores:
16%

SAT I Range (25th - 75th Percentile):
1030-1240

SAT I Verbal Range (25th – 75th Percentile):
510-620

SAT I Math Range (25th – 75th Percentile):
520-620

Retention Rate:
87.5%

SAT II Required?
Not for admission; the SAT II
Writing is used as a placement
exam for enrolled students.

**Top 10% of
High School Class:**
23%

Application Fee:
$55

Financial Information

In State Tuition:
$24,920

Room and Board:
$9,780

Books and Supplies:
$900

Personal Expenses:
$2,400

**Average Financial
Aid Package:**
$19,107
(including loans, work-study,
grants, and other sources)

**Students Who
Applied For Financial Aid:**
71%%

Students Who Received Aid:
62%

Financial Aid Forms Deadline:
February 15

Financial Aid Phone:
(415) 422-6303

Financial Aid Email:
finaid@usfca.edu

Financial Aid Website:
http://www.usfca.edu/acadserv/fi
naid/

Academics

The Lowdown On...
Academics

Degrees Awarded:
Bachelor's
Master's
Jurist Doctor
Doctor of Education

Most Popular Majors (Percentage of Students):
Business (36%)
Social Science (11%)
Psychologies (9%)
Communications (8%)
Nursing (7%)

Undergraduate Schools:
College of Arts and Sciences
McLaren College of Business
School of Nursing
College of Professional Studies

4 Year Graduation Rate:
47%

5 Year Graduation Rate:
63%

6 Year Graduation Rate:
66%

➜

Full-Time Faculty:
460

Faculty with Terminal Degree:
92%

Student-to-Faculty Ratio:
16 to 1

Average Course Load:
Four

Special Study Options

Dual Degree Program in Education, Enrichment Programs, Honors Program in the Humanities, Military Science/ROTC, Pre-health, Saint Ignatius Institute, Study Abroad, 3/2 Engineering, 4+3 Law Program

AP Test Score Requirements:

Possible credit for scores of 3, 4, or 5

IB Test Score Requirements:

Possible credit for scores of 4, 5, 6, or 7

Best Places to Study:

Gleeson Library, Crossroads and Lone Mountain

Sample Academic Clubs:

African and Latino Americans Empowered Pre-Health Alliance, American Marketing Association, Hospitality Management Association, National Society of Collegiate Scholars, Nursing Students Association, Pre-Dental, Psychology Society of Mind Klub, Society of Physics Students

Did You Know?

Sam Green, a lecturer in the media studies department, was nominated in 2004 for an Academy Award for his 2003 feature-length documentary, *The Weather Underground*.

McLaren College of Business is in the top 100 Best Undergraduate Business programs in the United States.

USF is in the top 10% of all academic institutions nationwide.

USF's FM radio station has won the Gavin Award as best college station in the U.S. four of the last seven years.

USF's student newspaper, The Foghorn, has won the Associated College Press' Newspaper of the Year (1998) and National Pacemaker awards for the last three years.

Students Speak Out On...
Academics

> "Those teachers in my major have been consistently wonderful; I have found a few boring lecturers in required classes (namely European History and Natural Science)."

Q "I have **good and bad teachers**. Some have inspired me to continue the course of study and some have inspired me to drop a class, but overall, they genuinely care about what they teach. That's what makes for interesting discussions and class participation."

Q "I would highly recommend the English and history departments; other than that, **I have mixed feelings.**"

Q "The teachers are **competent, fair, and understanding**. There are a lot with accents, too, so they can be hard to understand sometimes."

Q "Overall, the teachers are quite good. The young ones seem **genuinely eager to mold their students** into great people and the old ones seem comfortable in their well-worn-but-can't-miss routine."

Q "Teachers here are very devoted. From my experience, almost every teacher I've encountered has been **more than willing to help** me further my knowledge. I've developed strong bonds with many of my previous professors."

Q "More often than not, **the teachers are weird**. If not weird, they're definitely not normal. It's the teachers like ours that make it easier to see where all those idiosyncratic stories come from."

Q "The teachers I've had are **very helpful and flexible,** which is nice because it is more encouraging to succeed in a less cut-throat, deadline-oriented environment."

Q "The teachers are excellent. They come from diverse backgrounds and offer something unique for each class. Unlike my previous school, they are **very accessible and willing to talk** about anything, during their office hours, that is."

Q "The professors are mixed in terms of professionalism and skill. The core classes are generally boring and useless, which should be expected to a certain extent-but not in some instances. **The Honors Program is highly recommended** in terms of the valuable skills of analysis and contextualization it promotes, as well as the broad socio-historical dialogue it produces. I wouldn't suggest the Saint Ignatius Institute because they can seem overbearing at times."

Q "**Amazing!** My literature classes are filled with interesting and engaging texts, and my writing class is challenging, interesting, and engaging."

Q "The teachers are helpful, available, and friendly. They are **not exactly Harvard professors,** but they work hard to create an inspiring and thought-provoking environment."

Q "Most of the teachers I have had have been very encouraging to my own personal well-being and improvement as a writer; they have flexible office hours and are always more than happy to talk. Most of the teachers are **both excellent mentors as well as friends.**"

Q "I think the teachers are comparatively more accessible than the teachers at other universities. However, I find them to be **conservative in certain ways.**"

Q "The business professors are **pretty good** (especially finance), but the general education ones are mediocre."

Q "The teachers are knowledgeable and helpful-most of them exhibit **a real desire to be there** and to teach, which makes the experience more enjoyable for students."

The College Prowler Take On...
Academics

At a school like USF, academics often take a back seat to the city and often times, the religion preference of the school. But the professors at USF are one of the most important and inspirational parts of the complete university package. Because the school is relatively small, it is extremely easy to get to know your professors on a personal level. They are intriguing, dedicated, and passionate about their field and are more concerned with teaching than performing research. The best thing to do at USF is to take advantage of office hours and get to know the professors inside your major as well as outside.

Students at USF have many opportunities to concentrate their area of study and also to increase their challenges. With programs such as the Honors Program in the Humanities and the Saint Ignatius Institute, students can take more rigorous courses than the core curriculum and expand their academic horizons beyond their major. Also, USF provides a number of ways to make the most of your time in college, particularly with the Dual Degree Program in Education, which also regards studying abroad as important and makes it part of the required curriculum-something students value because any other dual degree program would not allow them the time to study abroad. Also, the 4+3 program enables students to take a minor in Legal Studies, and with appropriate LSAT scores, students are offered automatic admission into the USF Law School. The possibilities to succeed academically at USF are endless; students need to be aware of what is available and take advantage while they can.

B-

The College Prowler™ Grade on

Academics: B-

A high Academics grade generally indicates that professors are knowledgeable, accessible, and genuinely interested in their students' welfare. Other determining factors include class size, how well professors communicate, and whether or not classes are engaging.

Local Atmosphere

The Lowdown On...
Local Atmosphere

Region:
West

City, State:
San Francisco, CA

Setting:
Bay Area

Distance from Los Angeles:
6 hours

Distance from Lake Tahoe:
4 hours

Points of Interest:
Golden Gate Bridge
Alcatraz
Fisherman's Wharf
Chinatown
North Beach
Pacific Ocean
Union Square
Haight-Ashbury
Golden Gate Park
Presidio
Grace Cathedral

➜

Coit Tower

Mission

Castro

Cable Cars

Ghiradelli Square

San Francisco Opera House

City Hall

Japan Town

Closest
Shopping Malls:

Union Square

San Francisco Shopping Centre

Stonestown Mall

Movie Theatres:

AMC 1000 Van Ness

1000 Van Ness Avenue (at O'Farrell)

Phone: (415) 922-4262

AMC Kabuki 8

1881 Post Street, Japan Town

Phone: (415) 922-4262

United Artists Coronet

3575 Geary Blvd., Richmond

Phone: (415) 752-4400

Major Sports Teams:

49'ers (football)

Giants (baseball)

Five Fun Facts about San Francisco:

1. Golden Gate Park, established on April 4, 1870, is a man-made park that was built upon sand dunes and is 1,031 acres in size.

2. The infamous Cable Cars began running in 1873, originally with over eight different lines. San Francisco was the first city to ever use the Cable Car, but the Great Earthquake of 1906 damaged many of the lines. Today, some of the original lines built are still in use.

3. Alcatraz Island has a rich history; it was originally occupied by the military as a fort, then it was an army prison camp. Most notably, Alcatraz became the famous prison where the nation's worst criminals were sent, after which it became the site of the Native American peace community.

Now it is a part of the Golden Gate National Recreation Area, open with tours daily.

4. Mark Twain once said, "The coldest winter I ever saw was the summer I spent in San Francisco."

5. The historic streetcars, which run along Market Street and the Embarcadero to Fisherman's Wharf, began service in 1912. San Francisco has actual streetcars running from seven different countries and ten different cities across the United States.

Famous People:
Clint Eastwood, Jerry Garcia, Paul Desmond, Danny Glover, Robert Frost, Jack London, Joe DiMaggio, Merv Griffin, Benjamin Bratt, Josh Hartnett, James Hetfield, Kevin Pollak, Rob Schneider, O. J. Simpson, Jeffrey Tambor, and Robin Williams.

City Websites:
http://sanfrancisco.citysearch.com

http://www.sfvisitor.org

http://www.sfgate.com

http://ci.sf.ca.us/

Local Slang:
Hella - Extremely cool

Bridge and Tunnel People - Commuters into San Francisco from around the Bay Area

SoMa - South of Market Street; a popular area on the weekend, where bars and clubs seemingly pop up overnight

MUNI - The San Francisco Municipal Railway, better known as the city's bus lines

Tenderloin - Section of downtown notorious for being dangerous and unpleasant at night. Don't completely ignore it, though, because the Tenderloin has great restaurants and sites to see, but be careful and don't walk around there alone at night.

Students Speak Out On...
Local Atmosphere

"I love this city. There are a million things to do and a million little subcultures to get into. You can do all the touristy stuff your heart desires, and most of it is honestly worth doing. The city is the best part of being at USF."

Q "I feel really safe in San Francisco now, but in my first couple of years, when I didn't know the city as well, I was afraid to go to the Mission at night, walk through the Panhandle, and even down Divisadero. **I still won't go into Golden Gate Park alone at night**, or walk down around Market and Sixth and Seventh Streets."

Q "San Francisco has a fun and funky atmosphere where often anything goes! With this said, keep an open mind. **A wide array of cultural influences** allows students to explore world cuisine, languages, music, and even religion. Some students might take longer to adjust to such diversity, but they should be encouraged to broaden their cultural and philosophical horizons. Other universities are present but of little importance. SF State is sometimes good for the student in need of additional library resources, if nothing else. Fun attractions include classic streetcar and cable car rides, Alamo Square for all you Olsen Twins fans, Ocean Beach for twilight bonfires, and Baker Beach for the exhibitionist in us all."

Q "City life is **busy but incredibly fun**. Visit downtown, the parks, and the museums, but stay away from bad areas-like Hunter's Point, Tenderloin, and Mission Street at night."

Q "There are other universities around, but we don't have a rivalry or anything. There are three art schools, which make for a lot of **pretentiously dressed people in bars**. I've met Berkeley people through internships, but not really otherwise."

Q "San Francisco is an amazing town to go to school in. There is something here for everyone, and so many things are happening here; it's a great place to be. If you're coming here, **do the touristy stuff!** Go to Alcatraz, Fisherman's Wharf, and the Palace of the Fine Arts! It's a lot of fun and there is always something new to see or do."

Q "I love the city of San Francisco because there is something here for everyone. I don't like that there aren't a lot of other universities. **You have to be careful of certain parts** of the city like all cities. There's tons of stuff to visit, from museums to parks to restaurants to anything else."

Q "San Francisco has **a ton of stuff to see and experience**. SF State is another university not too far from here, but USF is the only one that is considered to be in the heart of the city."

Q "Excellent atmosphere; it's well-rounded in its mix of Big City, suburban, and coastal feel. I would stay away from the Tenderloin, SF State, and Daly City. I would recommend visiting **Golden Gate Park, Land's End, Mission Dolores, and Chinatown**."

Q "San Francisco is **my favorite city in the world**-it's laid back, fun, interesting, has history, and is just about every college student's dream."

Q "USF is all about the city atmosphere: **hectic, big, and exhilaratingly free**. There are other universities present, but we tend to be known as the snob of the collegiate group-definitely be a tourist! Yes, it can be overrated if you do it all the time, but you should act like one at least once because there's so much more to the city than college parties."

Q "The city of San Francisco is **very tolerant and liberal**. There are people of all walks of life here; college students (USF and others), adults, kids, everything."

Q "There is so much to see! The only thing I recommend avoiding is the Panhandle at night. The **beautiful places definitely outweigh the scary ones**."

Q "San Francisco has such a diverse culture, and it's a **very exciting place to be** in. There are various things to do in the city-plays, the Opera, ballet, concerts, parties, etc. The Bay Area boasts a number of distinguished universities like UC Berkeley, Stanford University, University of San Francisco, Mills College, San Francisco State University, and several community colleges. In such a fun, exciting, and cultured city-I can't think of anything to stay away from."

Q "The city is amazing, of course. Other universities are in San Francisco, but USF is snobbish and doesn't tend to intermingle. **Stay out of the Tenderloin at night**, and make sure to see all the best views and peruse all the great museums."

Q "The atmosphere is unlike any other place I have been. While San Francisco is a big city, it is not so big that you ever find yourself lost. Culturally, it is a diverse city and **a far cry from a traditional college town**, though there are quite a few schools inside its borders. I would recommend visiting the Museum of Modern Art, North Beach, Haight Street, the beaches, the Presidio, and the numerous independent theaters. Also, venture outside the city to places like the Marin Headlands, Sausalito, and the Napa Valley. Go everywhere you can!"

The College Prowler Take On...
Local Atmosphere

San Francisco is one of the most popular, gorgeous, and cosmopolitan cities in the world. Because of this, it is often the main reason students come to USF. There is always something to do in this city, whether it's checking out the latest restaurant, taking advantage of student discounts at the world-famous SF Opera and SF Ballet, walking through Golden Gate Park or across the Golden Gate Bridge, or enjoying a cultural stroll through the Mission, Chinatown, or North Beach. Everyone can find something about this city that they absolutely adore, but the most exciting part is the chance the city gives you to discover something new every day.

San Francisco, large and bustling as it may be, provides an excellent backdrop for the university. Whenever school becomes too stressful, students can always escape to their favorite off-campus site. Also, the abundance of history, beauty, and culture makes classroom activities more tangible and relevant; often classes take field trips to the city's museums or historical sites, as well as perform community service and work with the homeless. If you're looking for a fun, exciting, cultural, and hands-on experience, San Francisco is definitely the place to be.

The College Prowler™ Grade on

Local
Atmosphere: A

A high Local Atmosphere grade indicates that the area surrounding campus is safe and scenic. Other factors include nearby attractions, proximity to other schools, and the town's attitude toward students

Safety & Security

The Lowdown On...
Safety & Security

Number of USF Police:
Number of USF Public Safety Officers: 30

Phone: (415) 422-4222

Safety Services:
Emergency Phones, Emergency Response, Safety Presentations, Special Events, USF Alarms, Security Escort Service, Parking Enforcement, Campus Patrol, Campus Shuttle, Record Request

Health Clinic:
2235 Hayes Street, fifth floor, room nine (part of Sr. Mary Philippa Memorial Clinic)

Hours:
8:30 a.m.-5 p.m
walk-ins welcome

Services Provided:
Evaluation and treatment of acute illnesses and minor injuries, health education and evaluation of health concerns, nutritional counseling, smoking cessation counseling, stress management counseling, and education and evaluation of sexually transmitted diseases.

Students Speak Out On...
Safety & Security

"It's pretty good on campus, although it seems a little ridiculous at times. There were a couple of hate crimes and vandalisms this year, but they still haven't caught the people responsible."

Q "I have never felt unsafe on campus. It's open and **usually there are a lot of people around**, but there are also emergency poles. You push a button, and fifteen seconds later, security is there. Public Safety is great and dependable."

Q "USF is a **very secure** environment. I've never had a problem."

Q "Security is standard, but it proves to be good enough because the campus is not big and is in a good neighborhood. Plus, **you can always call Public Safety for an escort**, even if you're a few miles from campus."

Q "Very good, very organized. Although t**here isn't too much crime**, sometimes they seem a little over-prepared and eager."

Q "Public Safety kind of slacks off at times, but for the most part, I'd say the campus is **pretty safe**."

Q "Fairly good. We get **the occasional vagrant**, but they're pretty harmless. Nevertheless, it's easy (and bad) to forget that we are in a city, and there's always a measure of insecurity that comes with that."

Q "I don't think Public Safety has much of a **presence on campus**. I've only seen them occasionally, but I've never felt unsafe."

Q "I always feel **very safe on campus** and since September 11, the security has been more enforcing."

Q "USF has its own **University Public Safety**, and they are always looking out for the students' safety."

Q "Security hasn't been too good this semester. There have been quite a few robberies, particularly **people being threatened in the dark corners of the campus**. If you're going to be walking around in the dark, make sure you're accompanied by a large group of friends or call for an escort."

Q "The campus, while in the **middle of the city**, is well-protected and safe. It is close enough to everything that you can go anywhere, but it is secluded enough that you feel secure on campus."

Q "The campus is very secure with twenty-four-hour public safety, and there are dorm staff members **always on duty**."

Q "Recent criminal events have 'darkened' the campus's reputation as a safe and secure locale-be cautious after dark. Remember that San Francisco, like any major city, has **its share of hoodlums**. You might want to consider the university's free escort to get you home safe and sound after long study nights and campus events. Stay alert and always watch your back!"

The College Prowler Take On...
Safety & Security

USF Public Safety has an important influence on campus life. While some incidences are unavoidable and inevitable, Public Safety does its very best to give the campus and its students a safe, secure environment. Officers patrol the campus twenty-four hours a day. Both the campus shuttle and safety escorts are available to bring students to and from main campus, Loyola Village, Pedro Arrupe, and practically any place within the vicinity of campus.

Recent thefts and robberies on campus and in the dorms have been met with a quick response, due to the emergency poles strategically placed around campus and the fast action that results from calling the twenty-four-hour safety line. Also, whenever anything happens on campus, the word is spread almost instantaneously through the USF Connect emailing system. Keeping everyone aware of campus security breeches is one way Public Safety maintains a safe environment. Another way is through required ID checks at the entrance of every residence hall, though sometimes people (and their alcohol) sneak by because the checks are conducted by students. If anyone is caught drinking underage in the dorms, RA's will write a referral, but if a student is caught with drugs, Public Safety officers come immediately to handle of the situation.

The College Prowler™ Grade on

Safety & Security: B+

A high grade in Safety & Security means that students generally feel safe, campus police are visible, blue-light phones and escort services are readily available, and safety precautions are not overly necessary.

Computers

The Lowdown On...
Computers

High-Speed Network?
Yes

Wireless Network?
Yes

Number of Labs:
5

Number of Computers:
145

Operating Systems:
PC, MAC

Free Software:
Norton Anti-Virus

Discounted Software:
The only discounted software is sold in the bookstore or online at http://www.efollett.com. The company claims to sell the software at up to seventy-five percent off standard rates, so browse the website and compare prices.

24-Hour Labs:

UC Parina Computer Lab

Charge to Print?

Yes.

Did You Know?

While much of the administration uses MACs, the computer labs are dominated by PC's, with 134 of the computers using Windows and 11 of the computers equipped with the MAC server OS.

All computers on-campus are replaced every three years so that the equipment is up-to-date and in excellent shape.

Students Speak Out On...
Computers

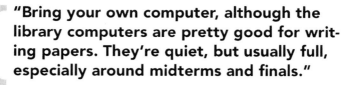

"Bring your own computer, although the library computers are pretty good for writing papers. They're quiet, but usually full, especially around midterms and finals."

Q "I brought my own computer, so I've never had a problem, but I have noticed that the library computers are usually taken and **the computer lab is always full**. If you know where to go and explore, there are open computers, like on the second floor of the library. They have Internet access and Microsoft Word, so if a research paper is due, you have all you need."

Q "The computer labs are **usually pretty full** and personal laptops are not allowed, but there are other places to bring your laptop on campus."

Q "No, you don't need your own computer. The computer labs are fairly crowded during the day, but you can always find at least one computer. **The network is great**; once you go Ethernet, you never want go back to anything slower."

Q "The computer network is great. We even have **wireless location**s."

Q "The university offers free Ethernet and dial-up (off campus) for all students. Although slow at times, it is **convenient and economical for the student budget**. The labs tend to fill up, so make sure you get there early if you need to print out materials. Laptop users will benefit from outlets found throughout the library. Definitely bring your own computer."

Q "You should definitely bring your own computer, but **be careful with laptops in dorms**. Things do get stolen."

Q "I would definitely advise bringing a computer of your own. The computer lab is **very crowded during lunch hour and during midterms and finals**, since many teachers assign projects or essays at those times. Plus, owning your own computer allows you to type up and print your papers at your convenience."

Q "There are several computer labs on campus, so you don't have to worry about bringing your own laptop to school. All the computers have **high-speed Internet** and programs that students need to use for class assignments."

Q "**You should bring a computer** because the labs get pretty crowded. They are always working on the network, so it is shut down pretty often."

Q "The computer network on campus is good-there is almost always a computer to use in the labs, and the fact that **there is a twenty-four-hour lab** is great! Some schools, I know, don't have that luxury. Also, the Internet is very speedy. Bringing your own computer is not a bad idea, particularly if you want to do work in your room, but it is not absolutely necessary."

Q "There are **tons of available computers on campus**, but they are often occupied. I'd recommend bringing a laptop."

Q "The network here is great, but there aren't enough computer labs. **Good luck trying to find an open computer** at lunchtime."

Q "I only had a computer for a year and it was more of a hassle because it was big, took up a lot of space, and was basically **useless and obsolete**. I ended up sharing with my roommate and using the lab computers, which have served me well. I would not worry about buying one if you don't already have one, considering whether or not you can work well in labs."

The College Prowler Take On...
Computers

USF provides a fast Ethernet service for all students and faculty on campus. The network is functional and has virtually no firewalls. If you bring your own computer, which is highly recommended due to the small number of computers available in the labs, be sure it has an Ethernet port. Don't worry if you don't have a cord because every dorm carries enough for each student. If you live off campus, USF will provide you with free dial-up service, which isn't very fast, but it helps cushion any student's budget.

ITS, the on-campus computer and network service, has a help desk and they are always more than happy to assist you with any questions or problems. They also maintain the computer labs and USF Connect, a source for student e-mail accounts, web registration, grades, and campus announcements. While most students come to school with their own private e-mail addresses, using the USF e-mail address is a smart idea. Most departments and professors send correspondence directly to USF accounts, so if you want to stay in touch with academics and campus events, be sure to check it often. USF Connect is easy to use, personalize, and it serves as an important new addition to the university's network.

The College Prowler™ Grade on

Computers: B

A high grade in Computers designates that computer labs are available, the computer network is easily accessible, and the campus' computing technology is up-to-date.

Facilities

The Lowdown On...
Facilities

Libraries:
2

Popular Places to Chill:
Crossroads
UC Parina Lounge
Harney Plaza
lawn in front of Gleeson Library

Student Center:
The University Center (UC)

Athletic Center:
Koret Recreation Center
Memorial Gymnasium

Campus Size:
55 acres

What Is There to Do On Campus?

Students at USF can grab an espresso or a smoothie on their way to class, grab a bite to eat in almost every building, work out or swim in an Olympic-sized pool, and hear live music before the sun sets. At night, students can study in the library atrium, check out a student production, or watch a movie on a silver screen in Harney Plaza.

Movie Theatre on Campus?

No, but there are often film events held around campus.

Bowling on Campus?

No.

Bar on Campus?

No.

Coffeehouse on Campus?

Yes. Crossroads at the University Center.

Favorite Things to Do:

During Dead Hour, most students eat lunch outside in Harney Plaza. On warmer days, or just days when it's not raining, the Plaza will feature a live band or DJ, giving students and faculty a musical interlude between classes. Vendors also use this popular plaza to sell items like jewelry, scarves, and handmade clothing. The computer labs, especially Parina, are always crowded and most students like to hang out in various locations in the UC to study and socialize.

Students Speak Out On...
Facilities

"The gym is great, even though I've only been three times in four years. My friend saw Danny Glover working out there."

Q "I think the facilities are nice. One thing I think we really need is a student transfer center for students that are interested in transferring into the school. I was a transfer student and **I found it incredibly hard to figure things out**. I have also talked with lots of other transfer students, and they hold the same frustrations about the school."

Q "USF has **good facilities**, a nice library, gym, and updates computers every three years."

Q "Everything here is **very up to date**. Computers, though I know nothing about them, are always speedy and easy to use, and the Koret Center facility is very nice. It has every kind of work out equipment anyone would ever need. The University Center is fun, too. It has a lounge, the cafeteria, Jamba Juice, and a café. I spend a lot of time there."

Q "The gym is really nice and big, and **the computer lab is okay**. Some of the buildings and facilities are nice, and others are not-so-new or nice."

Q "A variety of adequate facilities are available, most notably **an excellent gym**."

Q "Koret is **a beautiful, gigantic health center**, something to rave about in a big city like San Francisco. The computer labs and computers could be nicer or more high-tech, along with Parina Lounge, the campus common room."

Q "The computer facilities and student center are nothing to write home about, but the gym's **Olympic-sized pool** makes it one of the best fitness centers in the area."

Q "Everything is pretty nice, though sometimes things are **a little dingy in high-traffic areas**. For the most part, there's nothing to worry about."

Q "**The Koret Center is beautiful**, especially the swimming pool! The general appearance of the campus is very nice."

Q "We have a baseball field, an athletic track and field, and the gym is **well-equipped**."

Q "The facilities are good, for the most part. Some of the buildings are getting pretty old and a few of the elevators get stuck at times. However, it seems that **a lot of reno-vating is being done**, so hopefully that all will be taken care of soon. As for the athletic facilities-the student gym (Koret) is very nice; up-to date, well-kept. The library is a good building, though some books have to be sent from other libraries because the amount of books is lacking. A lot of work has been done to the University Center in the last couple years, though I'm not sure that it is worth it because students don't seem to be in there a ton. Perhaps more of that money could go to renovating the dorms and some of the older buildings."

Q "This school is pretty old, and for a Division I school, the facilities are **not good**."

The College Prowler Take On...
Facilities

USF is one of the most beautiful campuses in the world, with views of the Golden Gate Bridge, the San Francisco Bay, downtown, the Pacific Ocean, and the colorful city of San Francisco. All around campus, you'll find gorgeous flowers, trees, and exotic foliage. As far as buildings go, the majority of the campus is fairly old. Only the library, Koret Recreation Center, and Saint Ignatius Church appear new and refurbished; however, that is not to say the older buildings aren't aesthetically pleasing as well. The problem with the older buildings shows most on the inside. Students tend to complain that the dorms have an unpleasant odor and that the facilities are generally run-down or outdated.

The university recognizes that space is limited and renovations need to happen as quickly as possible. Currently, the UC, the Market cafeteria, and Lone Mountain Residence Hall are under construction, as well as a new wing for Phelan Hall. Future plans include remodeling the Memorial Gym, Campion Hall, Cowell Hall, Xavier Hall, the baseball field, and the Presentation Theater. In addition, the university wants to add desperately-needed parking spaces and to improve pedestrian walkways. While the future plans should bolt the campus into the twenty-first century, the process will be costly. With the tuition increase this year, many more can be expected as students feel the pain of costly renovations.

The College Prowler™ Grade on

Facilities: B

A high Facilities grade indicates that the campus is aesthetically pleasing and well-maintained; facilities are state-of-the-art, and libraries are exceptional. Other determining factors include the quality of both athletic and student centers and an abundance of things to do on campus.

Campus Dining

The Lowdown On...
Campus Dining

Freshman Meal Plan Requirement?
Yes.

Meal Plan Average Cost:
$3,600

Places to Grab a Bite with Your Meal Plan

Market
Location: UC second floor

Food: Various

Favorite Dish: Pizza, Cheese-burgers

Hours: Monday-Thursday 7 a.m.-8:30 p.m., Friday-Saturday 7 a.m.-7 p.m., Sunday 9:30 a.m.-8:30 p.m.

Lone Mountain Dining Hall
Location: Lone Mountain

Food: Various

Favorite Dish: Cheeseburgers

Hours: Monday-Thursday 8 a.m.-6 p.m., Friday 8 a.m.-2 p.m., Closed Saturday and Sunday

Hilltop Café

Location: Lone Mountain

Food: Sandwiches/Pastries/Coffee

Favorite Dish: Espresso

Hours: Monday-Thursday 8 a.m.-6 p.m., Friday 8 a.m.-2 p.m., Closed Saturday and Sunday

Crossroads

Location: UC first floor

Food: Coffee/Sandwiches/Pastries/Italian

Favorite Dish: Pizza

Hours: Monday-Friday 8 a.m.-8:30 p.m., Closed Saturday and Sunday

Jamba Juice

Location: UC first floor

Food: Smoothies

Favorite Dish: Razzmataz, Strawberries Wild

Hours: Monday-Thursday 8 a.m.-8 p.m., Friday 8 a.m.-2:30 p.m., Saturday 10 a.m.-3 p.m., Closed Sunday

Club Ed

Location: School of Ed., basement floor

Food: Sandwiches/Pastries

Favorite Dish: Bagels

Hours: Monday-Thursday 11:30 a.m.-8 p.m., Friday 11:30 a.m.-4:30 p.m., Saturday 7:30 a.m.-3 p.m., Closed Sunday

Off-Campus Places to Use Your Meal Plan:

None.

Student Favorites:

Jamba Juice, Crossroads

24-Hour On-Campus Eating?

No.

Did You Know?

Students used to be able to order pizza and other items with their meal plan from an off-campus site. Now, the only way to quench that pizza craving is to order one through the cafeteria. Plan ahead because the cafeteria closes early!

Students Speak Out On...
Campus Dining

"The cafeteria food is not too bad, but it's quite pricey. Crossroads and Jamba Juice are quite affordable, but, other than that, I would pack my lunch."

Q "The food is good, but **ridiculously expensive**. It doesn't make any sense."

Q "Food on campus isn't too bad, but just like anything else, **too much of it can get old really quickly**. There aren't any real differences in the food venues because they're all catered by one big mega-company. If you want less picked-over food, go to Lone Mountain Café."

Q "I don't really eat on campus-it's **too expensive!**"

Q "Apart from the deli, the food on campus is tasteless and unhealthy. **Make a b-line for the sandwich counter** if you desire an edible lunch-it's worth the wait and long lines. Be prepared: the deli closes early, so you might want to stock up for later."

Q "Food on campus is **horrible**, apart from Jamba Juice."

Q "The food at USF has improved exponentially over the past few years. There is enough variety that you don't feel it gets old. The cafeteria is **immaculate one day, filthy the next**; it's totally unpredictable."

Q "Campus food is good; however, a couple months with **the same menu can get tiring**. One can only take so many bagels, burritos, pre-made sandwiches, and pizza."

Q "One of my friends told me that USF has **the best cafeteria among schools in the Bay Area**. World Fare offers different kinds of food, ranging from Chinese, Western, Vegetarian, Fast Food, etc. They have fruits, juices, cereals, pastries, ice cream, and yogurt. The only drawback is that the food can be too expensive."

Q "It has gotten better over the last few years, though it is still overpriced. Jamba Juice is good, as is Crossroads. The dining halls have good food, but **the prices are too high**."

Q "It's better now, but more expensive. Everything is controlled by one cafeteria company, so there's n**ot much variety or difference in quality**, which is really too bad. There used to be a student-run coffee shop that was really comfortable and broken-in."

Q "The cafeteria is good and **a lot better than other schools** I've been too, but eventually you get sick of the same food every day. I like to order food with my roommate. We usually get Thai, Indian, or Chinese food, and it's delivered to the dorm, which is really convenient. Also, there are good restaurants if you go to Union Square. They're all over the place."

The College Prowler Take On...
Campus Dining

Campus dining at USF is a completely different experience than it was a mere three years ago. The new company, Bon Appetite, handles every single food-related franchise on campus. Sodexho-Marriott held the prior contract, and Bon Appetite is more than a mere step up. The food is way better, offers more options, and only organic items are used; however, the prices reflect the better quality. (Some say it's worth it, though.) Because USF is a relatively small school, there are only a handful of places to eat. The main cafeteria is the Market, located in the University Center-at the heart of campus, which means it is insanely crowded at lunch and dinner time. Unfortunately, all of the dining services on campus close at abnormal hours. If you live in Lone Mountain, be prepared to hike down the mountain to main campus for food because the dining hall there is closed on the weekends.

Most students complain about the food on campus, but the reality is that dissatisfaction comes from repetition. Expect to get sick of dining hall food, no matter what school you go to. Fortunately, San Francisco has a million excellent restaurants, so you can always take a break from campus dining and check out the latest taqueria or bistro. Here's one last bit of advice: the meal plan at USF is a declining balance, which means most people spend all of their money at the beginning of the semester. Be sure to ration a weekly amount and stick to it!

B

The College Prowler™ Grade on

Campus Dining: B

Our grade on Campus Dining addresses the quality of both school-owned dining halls and independent on-campus restaurants as well as the price, availability, and variety of food.

Off-Campus Dining

The Lowdown On...
Off-Campus Dining

Restaurant Prowler: Popular Places to Eat!

Beach Chalet

Food: American/Traditional

Address: 1000 Great Highway, Ocean Beach

Phone: (415) 386-8439

Cool Features: Microbrewery on location, priceless view of the Pacific Ocean, live music, and downstairs is the Golden Gate Park Visitor's Center, with murals, mosaics, and wood carvings done in 1936 as part of the federal works program.

Also, this restaurant is one of the few places in the city with a parking lot.

Price: $20 per person

Hours: Friday-Saturday 9 a.m.-12 a.m., Sunday-Thursday 9 a.m.-11 p.m.

Blue Front Café

Food: Deli/Mediterranean

Address: 1430 Haight Street

Phone: (415) 252-5917

Price: $10 and under per person

Hours: Sundays-Thursdays 7:30 a.m.-10 p.m., Friday and Saturday 7:30 a.m.-11 p.m.

→

Cinderella's Bakery, Delicatessen, and Restaurant

Food: Russian

Address: 436 Balboa Street, Richmond

Phone: (415) 751-9690

Price: $15 and under per person

Hours: Tuesday-Saturday 9 a.m.-9 p.m., Sunday 9 a.m.-7 p.m.

Equinox

Food: American

Address: 5 Embarcadero Center, Downtown

Phone: (415) 788-1234

Cool Features: Northern California's only revolving rooftop restaurant and cocktail lounge that makes a complete 360-degree revolution every 45 minutes. The restaurant offers spectacular views of the San Francisco bay and the sparkling city skyline.

Price: $20-30 dollars per person; $15 and under per person for dessert (worth the view, at least once!)

Hours: Sunday-Thursday 5 p.m.-11 p.m., Friday-Saturday 5 p.m.-1 a.m.

Foreign Cinema

Food: Mediterranean/French/Californian

Address: 2534 Mission Street, Mission District

Phone: (415) 648-7600

Cool Features: Fireplace, outdoor dining, and foreign films shown on a large concrete wall during dining hours. See http://www.foreigncinema.com/film.html for current film listings.

Price: $30 per person

Hours: Tuesday-Thursday 5:30 p.m.-10 p.m., Friday-Saturday 5:30 p.m.-11 p.m., Sunday 11 a.m.-9 p.m.

Frjtz

Food: Belgian

Address: 579 Hayes Street

Phone: (415) 864-7654

Cool Features: Frjtz serves crepes and Belgian fries with fifteen types of dipping sauces, such as balsamic mayo and curry ketchup. Frjtz is also a self-proclaimed "DJ art teahouse."

Price: $15 and under per person

Hours: Monday-Thursday 8 a.m.-10 p.m.; Friday-Saturday 8 a.m.-12 a.m.; Sunday 8 a.m.-9 p.m.

Fruitful Grounds

Food: Sandwiches/Salads/Mediterranean

Address: 1813 Fulton Street, USF area

Phone: (415) 221-1876

Price: $10 and under per person

Hours: Monday-Thursday 7 a.m.-7 p.m., Friday-Sunday 8 a.m.-6 p.m.

The Grove

Food: American/Californian/Coffeehouse

Address: 2016 Fillmore Street, Fillmore

Phone: (415) 474-1419

Price: $15 and under per person

Hours: Daily 7 a.m.-11p.m.

Mel's Drive-In

Food: American

Address: 3355 Geary Blvd., Richmond

Phone: (415) 387-2244

Cool Features: Mel's is a vintage 1950's coffee shop open late and modeled after the original Mel's featured in "American Graffiti."

Price: $10 and under per person

Hours: Sunday-Thursday 6 a.m.-1 a.m., Friday-Saturday 6 a.m.-3 a.m.

Naan 'n Curry

Food: Indian/Pakistani

Address: 642 Irving, Inner Sunset

Phone: (415) 664-7225

Price: $15 and under per person

Hours: Daily 11:30 a.m.-12 a.m.

Ploy II Thai Cuisine

Food: Thai

Address: 1770 Haight Street

Phone: (415) 387-9224

Price: $10 and under per person

Hours: Daily 4 p.m.-10 p.m., Tuesday-Saturday 11:30 a.m.-3 p.m.

The Pork Store

Food: American/Breakfast

Address: 1451 Haight Street

Phone: (415) 864-6981

Price: $10 and under per person

Hours: Monday-Friday 7 a.m.-3:30 p.m., Saturday-Sunday 8 a.m.-4 p.m.

Pluto's

Food: American

Address: 627 Irving Street, Inner Sunset

Phone: (415) 753-8867

Cool Features: Fresh, made to order food as well as roasted turkey, stuffing, and cranberry sauce…like Thanksgiving all year long!

Price: $10 and under per person

Hours: Daily 11 a.m.-11 p.m.

Q

Food: Traditional American/Californian

Address: 225 Clement, Richmond

Phone: (415) 752-2298

Cool Features: Childhood favorites (like Macaroni and Cheese with Tater Tots) with a stylish flare.

Price: $15 and under per person

Hours: Daily 11:30 a.m.-3 p.m., 5 p.m.-11 p.m.

The Stinking Rose

Food: Italian

Address: 325 Columbus Avenue, North Beach

Phone: (415) 781-7673

Price: $25 and under per person

Hours: Sunday-Thursday 11 a.m.-11 p.m., Friday-Saturday 11 a.m.-12 a.m.

Straits Café

Food: Singaporean/Pan-Asian

Address: 3300 Geary Blvd., Richmond

Phone: (415) 668-1783

Price: $25 and under per person

Hours: Monday-Thursday 11:30 a.m.-3 p.m. and 5 p.m.-10 p.m., Friday-Saturday 11:30 a.m.-11 p.m., Sunday 4 p.m.-10 p.m.

Tommy's Authentic Mexican Restaurant

Food: Mexican

Address: 5929 Geary Blvd., Richmond

Phone: (415) 387-4747

Price: $15 and under per person

Hours: Wednesday-Monday 11 a.m.-11 p.m.

Student Favorites:

Best of Thai

Mel's

Frjtz

Pancho's

Taqueria Balazo

Blue Front Café

The Pork Store

Late-Night Dining:

Mel's

A Taste of Thai

Frjtz

24-Hour Eating:

Lucky Penny

Mr. Pizza Man

Denny's

Video Café 24 Hours

Closest Grocery Stores:

Albertson's

1750 Fulton Street at Masonic

Phone: (415) 923-6411

Cala Foods

4041 Geary Blvd. at Fifth Avenue

Phone: (415) 221-9191

Safeway

735 Seventh Ave. at Fulton

Phone: (415) 752-4073

Best Pizza:
Nizario's
Bella Pizza
Village Pizzeria
Blondie's
Fat Slice

Best Chinese:
Yank Sing
Ho's

Best Breakfast:
The Pork Store
Mel's

Best Healthy:
Pluto's
Whole Foods Market

Best Place to Take Your Parents:
Beach Chalet
Equinox

Did You Know?

San Francisco is famous for Rice-a-Roni, fresh seafood, Ghiradelli chocolate, and sourdough bread.

Like clam chowder? San Francisco has the best chowder on the Pacific coast. Try it in a sourdough bread bowl!

Food is a celebration in San Francisco, with festivals year round honoring everything from beer to chocolate to crab.

Students Speak Out On...
Off-Campus Dining

"The Twilight Cafe is the best bet near campus, as well as a handful of restaurants nearby on Geary or, for the most adventurous, Haight Street-like Taqueria Balazo."

Q "You must go to Tony's Cable Car restaurant on Masonic and Geary-awesome burgers. Pancho's on Geary and Stanyan has excellent Mexican food. Mel's is great for late night/morning good old American food. Pizza Orgasmica on **Clement between Ninth and Tenth is a fun place** to get some great pizza and have a few drinks at the bar. Café Riggio and Café Tiramisu are yummy Italian restaurants, but only go if you have money to splurge. Union square has lots of restaurants, like Cheesecake Factory on top of Macy's, and Clement is a good place to go for cheap stores with anything you want and cheap pork buns! There are lots of Chinese restaurants there as well."

Q "San Francisco has **really good places to eat**. A few include: a small and cheap Russian café called Cinderella's, Indonesian and Thai restaurants just a few blocks away (Thai Café, Bali Café, Bamboo Village, Straits Café), and so many more if you're willing to commute around the city."

Q "The food is good. There are all different types of restaurants, so you should be able to find what you want. Also, **the prices are reasonable**. Some good places are Zona Rosa, Fat Slice Pizza (both on Haight), Pancho's, Nizarrio's Pizza, The Best in Thai Food, Best of Thai, Mel's Diner, as well as a bunch of places on Clement Street, Geary Street, Haight Street, and North Beach."

Q "Immediately near campus, there are a few good places. Nani's Coffee on Geary is new and wonderful. Pancho's is a pretty good taqueria down the street. **Fruitful Grounds is the closest lunch café**, right by Filthy's (the liquor store). They're pretty good, but their frappucino things suck."

Q "**If you want to eat good food**, one of the best places in America is San Francisco. I think they have the most restaurants a city can have and the most variety, too. One of my favorite places is Burma Super Star, near Clement and Fifth. It serves Burmese food. Ask for the leeche smoothie. For Indian food, my favorite place is the Indian Clay Oven on Fillmore and Haight. The mango lassis and the chicken tikka Marsala is to die for and so is the nann bread."

Q "SF is filled with thousands of incredible places to eat! At **every price range you can imagine** and for every taste to satisfy. Any place in North Beach is amazing. Haight Street is known for a few good places as well."

Q "Restaurants off campus are fabulous. There is **a huge variety of food within ten minutes walking distance** of campus-great sushi, great pizza, great Chinese, great Thai, great Middle Eastern, you name it. Check out Sushi Boom, Fat Slice, and Best of Thai."

Q "There are **a lot of restaurants** kind of by school, on Geary-Hukilau (Hawaiian food) is pretty good."

Q "San Francisco has a reputation for some of the best food in the world, so off-campus restaurants are excellent. **From Russian to Thai and even Spanish cuisine, the City has it all!** A variety of local haunts are available to settle your exotic craving for papusas, pelmeni, and paella. Near campus dining includes Taqueria Balazo (Mexican food on Haight Street for spicy South-of-the-Border delights), Mel's Diner (traditional 1950s American fare-an experience you'll never forget), Arguello Market (fresh salads and hand-carved sandwiches), and Cinderella Bakery (Russian dinners and pastries that keep the local 'comrades' coming back for more). Restaurants in the Richmond District offer more options. Pacific Café is a 'City secret' that serves up the freshest, most delicious seafood the Bay has to offer. Golden Gate Park's famous Beach Chalet dishes up California cuisine and microbrews with great views of Ocean Beach and the roaring Pacific. Clement Street, the City's unofficial 'second Chinatown,' is lined with Asian, French, and Russian selections all within walking distance to USF."

Q "San Francisco has almost every kind of restaurant. I like Best of Thai on Haight Street because it's **fast, tasty, cheap**, and big enough for two people."

Q "The off-campus area is all about restaurants-cafés, luncheons, bistros, diners-**it's all pretty good**. So much food, so little time. Good spots? It's difficult to say…maybe Tommy's, Cheesecake Factory, Melissa's, Askew Grill, Hukilau, Sushi Boom, Shanghai 1930, Calzones, The Stinking Rose, Fruitful Grounds, and Nizario's."

The College Prowler Take On...
Off-Campus Dining

San Francisco is one of the greatest cities for dining out, where you can find any kind of restaurant that will fit every kind of budget. You just have to have an open mind and an empty stomach! Many districts in the city specialize in certain types of food, like North Beach for exceptional Italian, Chinatown for Chinese, the Mission for the greatest Mexican food, or the Wharf for outstanding seafood; the possibilities are endless. On one street alone, you can find Thai restaurants next to Chinese noodle houses across from Russian bakeries next to Korean BBQ houses above Mexican cantinas behind Moroccan restaurants and hookah lounges (Case in point: Geary Blvd.). All of the choices San Francisco has to offer make it really hard to choose favorites. The best advice for finding a handful of great places to check out would be to ask five people for their favorite restaurants, and then you'll probably get five different answers; all of which are worth a visit.

Eating off-campus is very popular at USF, not only because the campus dining is expensive and mediocre, but because taking advantage of what the City has to offer is a favorite past-time of most students. Around campus, there are many areas dense with options, like Haight Street and Geary Blvd. The only downside is that eating out and sampling all of the options at hand can become costly, but for the motivated and budgeted, anything is possible.

The College Prowler™ Grade on

Off-Campus Dining: A

A high off-campus dining grade implies that off-campus restaurants are affordable, accessible, and worth visiting. Other factors include the variety of cuisine and the availability of alternative options (vegetarian, vegan, Kosher, etc.).

Campus Housing

The Lowdown On...
Campus Housing

Room Types:
Small Double Room, Standard Double Room, Large Double Room, Small Single Room, Large Single Room

Best Dorms:
Lone Mountain, Loyola Village

Worst Dorms:
Phelan, Pedro Arrupe

Dormitories:

Gillson Hall
Floors: 8
Total Occupancy: 368
Bathrooms: Shared by Floor

Co-Ed: Yes
Percentage of Men/Women: 40% Men/60% Women
Percentage of First-Year Students: 100%
Room Types: Standard Double Rooms
Special Features: Recreation Area, Piano, Pool Table, Vending Machines, Common Kitchen, Television Room, Laundry

Hayes-Healy
Floors: 8
Total Occupancy: 375
Bathrooms: Shared by Floor
Co-Ed: Yes
Percentage of Men/Women:

➜

40% Men/60% Women
Percentage of First-Year Students: 100%
Room Types: Standard Double Rooms
Special Features: Recreation Area, Pool Table, Ping-Pong Table, Vending Machines, Common Kitchen, and Laundry. Hayes-Healy also houses the Martin-Baro Scholars learning and living program.

Lone Mountain

Floors: 4
Total Occupancy: 174
Bathrooms: Shared by Floor
Co-Ed: Yes
Percentage of Men/Women: 40% Men/60% Women
Percentage of First-Year Students: 0%
Room Types: Small Single Rooms, Large Double Rooms
Special Features: Common Kitchen, Laundry, Dining Hall, Television Lounge, Pool Table, Global Living Community.

Pedro Arrupe Hall

Floors: 4
Total Occupancy: 102
Bathrooms: Shared by Floor
Co-Ed: Yes
Percentage of Men/Women: 40% Men/60% Women
Percentage of First-Year Students: 0%
Room Types: Small Double Rooms, Standard Double Rooms, Small Single Rooms
Special Features: Common Kitchen, Laundry, Justice Education Community.

Phelan Hall

Floors: 5

Total Occupancy: 492
Bathrooms: Shared by Floor
Co-Ed: Yes, with the option of same-sex floors
Percentage of Men/Women: 40% Men/60% Women
Percentage of First-Year Students: 10%
Room Types: Small Double Rooms, Double Rooms, Large Single Rooms
Special Features: Multipurpose Lounge, Television Lounge, Common Kitchen, Laundry, ATM Machine, Phelan Multicultural Community, Erasmus Project, Saint Ignatius Institute, Office of Residence Life, University Bookstore, KDNZ and KUSF (the campus radio stations), Residence Hall Association offices, and the Foghorn offices.

Xavier Hall

Floors: 4
Total Occupancy: 176
Bathrooms: Shared by Floor
Co-Ed: No, all women
Percentage of Men/Women: 0%/100%
Percentage of First-Year Students: 50%
Room Types: Standard Double Rooms, Large Single Rooms
Special Features: Garden Kitchen shared with University Ministry, Laundry, Women's Resource Center, Television Lounge, In-Room Sinks

Community Apartments

Fulton House
Floors: 2
Total Occupancy: 12
Bathrooms: In-Room
Co-Ed: No, all women

Percentage of Men/Women: 0% Men/100% Women
Percentage of First-Year Students: 0%
Room Types: Standard Double Rooms, Large Double Rooms, Small Single Rooms
Special Features: Full Kitchen, Washer and Dryer, Furnished Living Room, Bedrooms, and Dining Room

Loyola Village
Floors: 4
Total Occupancy: 343
Bathrooms: In-Room
Co-Ed: Yes
Percentage of Men/Women: 40% Men/60% Women
Percentage of First-Year Students: 0%
Room Types: Apartment

Standard, Large, and Ex-Large Rooms
Special Features: Dishwasher, Garbage Disposal, Refrigerator, Electric Stove, Microwave Oven, Community Television Room, Copy Machine, Laundry

Undergrads Living on Campus: 50%

Number of Dormitories:
6

Number of University Owned Apartments:
2

Available for Rent
Refrigerators, Freezers, and Microwaves

Bed Type
Extra-long Twin (with option to bunk)

Cleaning Service?
In public areas only. Students residing in Community Apartments are responsible for cleaning their own bathrooms.

What You Get

Bed, Ethernet cord and connection, cable TV jack, desk and chair, desk lamp, closet or wardrobe, dresser (often built into the closet), mirror, window blinds, bookshelf, and telephone with voicemail and free campus and local calls. The apartment-style dorms come fully furnished as well, which includes everything above in addition to living-room furniture.

Also Available

All dorms and apartments are smoke-free; Special-Interest Housing and Learning-Learning communities are available: Erasmus Project, Saint Ignatius Institute, Phelan Multicultural Community, Pedro Arrupe Justice Education Community, Global Living Community, and the Martin-Baro Scholars Program.

Did You Know?

USF originally built Loyola Village to house faculty members and their families. Fortunately, the Village did not sell out, and the university converted the rest of the town homes into excellent and convenient student housing.

Students Speak Out On...
Campus Housing

{ **"I think they've re-done the dorms since I lived in them. Lone Mountain is kind of isolated, but it has great views, and I've always wanted to live there."**

○ "I live in Xavier and I love it. **I have a view of the ocean**, I have a sink in my room, and it's quiet when I need to study. I avoided Gillson and Hayes-Healy because they are the freshmen dorms, and there is a ton of partying in them. I have friends who like to find refuge in my room when they need to do homework because the dorm they live in is too crazy for them to get anything accomplished."

○ "I think the dorms are nice, even though a lot of people think they aren't. I used to go to a state school, and those have some nasty dorms. The best dorm I would say is Lone Mountain. Some say it is **like a resort**, though it may have changed now that they have let all the sophomores in there. It is a very nice, quiet, and clean place with awesome views on the north side that used to only house upperclassmen."

○ "Dorms are a good thing to experience. You get to meet all the students your age, and most likely that's where you will meet many of the friends that will stick with you after graduation. Make sure to **bring shower slippers and a small fridge**, if you can find one. Renting them isn't too expensive, though."

○ "My dorm is okay; it's off-campus, and it has transfer students. **Loyola Village is nice but pricey**."

Q "Dorms are cool but get old after the second year. While they are good for social networking, it's difficult to deal with no privacy and minimal personal space constantly. It's very much like living in the public eye. Here's the breakdown: Gillson is a refurbished freshmen dorm, Hayes-Healy is also a freshmen dorm, but it's still pretty clean and, like Gillson, it can be very loud and social. Phelan is loud and in the middle of everything, but it is also really big and impersonal. **Lone Mountain is older and much quieter** because it's secluded. Xavier is all girls; Pedro is too far and too cruddy, and Loyola Village is cool but also very impersonal."

Q "The dorms are standard. Phelan ranks as the worst, most filthy living experience in San Francisco, save Haight Street. **I would recommend Lone Mountain** or Loyola Village student apartments as top choices."

Q "**The dorms are fair**. Lone Mountain is good; Gillson and Phelan are bad."

Q "Loyola Village is the place to be! Apartment and townhouse style, the two-year old complex is hardly a dorm. I've never had the experience of living anywhere else though, so I'd say Hayes-Healy and the freshmen halls are going to be **stereotypical dorm-style housing**."

Q "**The sophomore dorms smell**, but it's good to live in the residence halls for the great experience. Lone Mountain is great, clean, and fairly big."

Q "The dorms are dorms. They're not very big, but they do the job. Xavier Hall has some pretty nice rooms (and sinks in the rooms), and Phelan is alright. Loyola Village has really nice, new apartments, though they're quite expensive-**you can probably find cheaper places off campus**, but they probably won't be as convenient or come with furniture."

Q "The newly built Loyola Village dorms are nice. Older dorms, like Xavier and Phelan, **should really be renovated**."

The College Prowler Take On...
Campus Housing

Living on campus is one of the most important experiences any college student can have. Most students make life-long friends from their roommates and hall-mates, as well as share in the experience of all-nighters and group study sessions together. As any student can tell you, living on campus is also incredibly convenient; all you have to do is wake up five minutes before class and you'll still make it on time. At USF, freshmen and sophomores are required to live on campus, unless they are residents of San Francisco or the Bay Area. Since the majority of USF students are not local, the amount of underclassmen on campus is overwhelmingly high. There are two dorms designated as freshmen-only and one dorm entirely made of sophomores, which is great for meeting and making friends. Also, USF has many learning-living communities, which allow students to live with their fellow classmates, who share the same goals and interests. The living-learning communities also enrich the experience of college life, as well as make it easier to get the notes if you miss a class.

The biggest complaint about campus housing at USF is the quality of the dorm buildings. Hayes-Healy, Gillson, Phelan, Xavier, and Lone Mountain are practically ancient and often smell like it. The good news is that by the time junior and senior year come around, students can move off campus or live in Loyola Village-the newly built apartment-style residences. Most students rave about the quality of life in Loyola Village because the buildings are even newer, furnished, and in better shape than most places in the city. Regardless of where you live, the experience in residence halls at USF can always be seen as fun and social. It's all what you make of it.

The College Prowler™ Grade on
Campus Housing: B+

A high Campus Housing grade indicates that dorms are clean, well-maintained, and spacious. Other determining factors include variety of dorms, proximity to classes, and social atmosphere.

Off-Campus Housing

The Lowdown On...
Off-Campus Housing

Undergrads in Off-Campus Housing:
50%

Average Rent for...
Studio: $900-$1,200
1BR: $1,250-$1,600
2BR: $1600-$2100

Assistance Contact:

Julie Orio, Assistant Director of Apartment Life and Off-Campus Housing

Web: usfca.edu/residence_life/offcampus/index.html

Phone: (415) 422-6824

E-mail: orl@usfca.edu

Popular Areas:

Richmond

Around USF

Sunset

Students Speak Out On...
Off-Campus Housing

"Off-campus housing is very convenient and is about the same price as dorms and a lot more comfortable. It is definitely worth it, and the student bus pass makes for easy travel to and from off-campus housing."

"It can be expensive, but it's really worth it. It's gotten **cheaper and more available** in the past couple years, and the neighborhoods are mostly all really nice and quiet, especially west of campus."

"I think it can be convenient, but it is scary to even begin looking for a place in such a big city. I think living on campus is really the way to go, although **living off can be more affordable**."

"Housing off campus is definitely worth it! It's **affordable, by San Francisco standards**, if you share an apartment with roommates, which is a fun way to live anyway when you are young."

"I never tried it. If you manage to get a place near campus, then you're set since anywhere else is too far of a walk and **parking is horrible!**"

"Yes, it's worth it, especially if you can **get a couple of other roommates**. In fact, it can be much cheaper than living on campus."

Q "Off-campus housing is **convenient but very costly**. San Francisco is the most expensive city in the nation in terms of housing, so shop around for the best prices! Availability and rates constantly fluctuate, so keep up on listings; http://www.craigslist.com is a great resource for finding the perfect student apartment. Students on a budget might want to consider one or more roommates. All in all, an apartment is probably the best option for living and great for guests and entertaining!"

Q "It is a pain in the butt! On-campus apartments, or in other words Loyola Village, are **really nice but pricey**."

Q "It's not convenient to live off campus because the exemption process to get off campus, if you're a freshman or sophomore, is very strict. However, if exempt, apartment living is **more spacious and convenient** for get-togethers, cooking, etc."

Q "Finding a place is easy, if you look hard enough. It's **absolutely worth it** because USF housing is way too pricey."

Q "Housing off campus is fine, but make sure you have your friends picked out and lined up before that because you won't be seeing much of campus and new people after you move off. A word to the wise: just **don't move too far away from campus** because you'll never go to class."

The College Prowler Take On...
Off-Campus Housing

San Francisco is one of the most expensive cities in the world to live in. The average rent is well over $1,000, and finding a place is almost as hard as paying for it. However expensive the place may be, living in the dorms will most likely be just as costly, if not more. Fortunately, though, over the past few years, the renting prices have gone down, but they're still not low enough to fit the average college student's income level. If you're set on living off campus after your sophomore year, as all freshmen and sopho- mores are required to live on campus, then finding a roommate (or two, or three) is the most cost-efficient way to afford living in the City. Finding a roommate isn't too hard, especially because the Residence Life office has a special division for off-campus living and their website features a listing of USF students looking for roommates. There are always flyers around, cluttering the bathrooms and other public places, describing rooms for rent and roommates desired.

The most popular neighborhoods for USF students living off campus are the Richmond (especially right around USF and along Geary Blvd.) and the Sunset, though San Francisco is small enough for students to live in any area and still be within a few miles of campus. If you're adventurous, you can walk to school from most areas, and you'll still always have the MUNI bus lines. The downside to taking MUNI if you live farther away is that you'll be leaving for school at least an hour before you need to be there. (Try to find a roommate with a car). Of course, living off campus has its perks, too, like having your own kitchen, a quiet and private place to relax or study, and easy access to your favorite neighborhood stores, restaurants, and cafés.

The College Prowler™ Grade on

Off-Campus Housing: B-

A high grade in Off-Campus Housing indicates that apartments are of high quality, close to campus, affordable, and easy to secure.

Diversity

The Lowdown On...
Diversity

American Indian:
1%

Asian or Pacific Islander:
26%

African American:
6%

Hispanic:
14%

White:
36%

International:
6%

Out-of-State:
30%

Unknown:
2%

Political Activity:
Due to San Francisco's liberal reputation, most of the students at USF are drawn to the liberal atmosphere. Social Justice is part of the school's motto; this can be seen particularly in its endorsement of students protesting the School of the Americas and the war in Iraq. While there are many radical extremists in the student body at USF, there are also some conservative ones. Like most schools, much of the student body remains silent or apathetic regarding political views.

Gay Tolerance:
Like San Francisco, USF is safe and accepting of its gay population. Not only are the students encouraged to be open about their sexuality, but faculty members are encouraged just as well. This support provides evidence that USF prides itself on its acceptance, promotion, and advancement of diversity.

Most Popular Religions:
All religions are represented throughout campus, though there is a significant, though not predominant, number of Catholics. This is because the school itself is Catholic. St. Ignatius Church is on campus, and it is also the site of the graduation ceremony.

Economic Status:
USF has students from diverse economic backgrounds, but there seems to be a good number of wealthy students, due in part to the expensive tuition. Some students complain about all the "rich kids."

Minority Clubs:
As USF is one of the most diverse universities in the United States, it supports the notion that minorities should be a strong and vital force on campus. There are at least ten official clubs and fraternities designated "cultural," while many more exist unofficially. A sampling of some of the minority clubs that are active at USF follows: Black Student Union, Chinese Student Union, Kasamahan (the Filipino-American Student Association), PEACE Partners (People of Color Enhancing Advancement in the College Environment), and Hui O' Hawaii. For a complete list of minority clubs, please visit the Multicultural Student Services site at http://www.usfca.edu/mcss

Students Speak Out On...
Diversity

"It's so diverse. I love it. There's this whole contingent from Guam, and I love everyone I've met-where else would that happen off of Guam? I'm from a really white town, and my experiences here have been so great."

"It is pretty diverse-apparently it is **one of the twenty most diverse campuses in the country**. That's cool, because you can get a better perspective on things, and it can help you to understand other points of view, as well as possibly change yours, if you let it."

"I don't think the campus is as diverse as everyone says. There are **a lot of cliques**, though, and reverse discrimination."

"I'd say it's as diverse as it can get. After all, **it's in San Francisco!**"

"The University's diversity is average, but in a city like San Francisco, which offers **the cultures of the world**, finding your own cultural or racial niche shouldn't be too difficult. On campus, the more diverse students tend to be drawn to subjects that reflect their own respective cultures."

"The campus is **mostly white and Asian**, with a limited black and Hispanic population."

Q "This school is **very diverse**. One of my favorite things about USF is its diversity."

Q "It's quite diverse. Caucasians are still the dominant ones on campus, but there is also **a decent number of different international students** from all over the world."

Q "The campus is fairly diverse, with notable Asian, Hispanic, and black student populations, most of which have their own social clubs and organizations. At times, USF appears as **a culture rainbow** of yellow, brown, and white blending together in Social Justice harmony."

Q "There are many different ethnicities represented at USF, but **each group seems to stick with their own**. While there is no apparent racial tension, I wish people would blend together more and let down their social barriers."

The College Prowler Take On...
Diversity

Ranked as one of the top twenty diverse universities in the nation, USF is a hub for ethnic and international flare. Like the city of San Francisco, USF caters to all religions (despite being a Jesuit university) and all races. The variety of students you will find at USF emulates the school's motto of embracing and accepting diversity. The diversity on this campus can open your mind and help to make you see things in a different light. It can also fuel your thinking; you may find yourself thinking about things you never knew existed or thinking in ways you never thought possible. Most students take advantage of this diversity by joining the numerous cultural clubs and organizations at hand. Learning about different cultures at USF happens outside the classroom just as easily as inside the classroom.

While some might find the abundance of ethnicity overwhelming, there tends to be very few clashes or conflicts, and at the same time, lots of intermixing. Other universities and areas of high diversity find their representative groups remaining closely tied and exclusive, but at USF, anyone and everyone is welcome to celebrate and participate in all aspects of each cultural experience available.

A-

The College Prowler™ Grade on

Diversity: A-

A high grade in Diversity indicates that ethnic minorities and international students have a notable presence on campus and that students of different economic backgrounds, religious beliefs, and sexual preferences are well-represented.

Guys & Girls

The Lowdown On...
Guys & Girls

Men Undergrads:
35%

Women Undergrads:
65%

Birth Control Available?
No.

Most Prevalent STDs on Campus:
Genital Herpes and Genital Warts

Social Scene:

The residence halls are social central at USF, particularly because all underclassmen are required to live on campus. Each residence hall has an RHA (Residence Hall Association) representative that works with the Resident Advisors to put on special events and socials. Plus, living on campus at a relatively small school allows you to make a solid base of friends that will carry over after everyone has moved off campus. Also, getting involved in clubs and organizations on campus, as well as studying in the UC or in Harney Plaza, are great ways for students at USF to meet and mingle with each other.

Hookups or Relationships?

More often than not, those students at USF that are dating are involved in relationships; however, random hookups on college campuses are inevitable. On warm days, you'll see couples, along with everyone else, basking in the sunlight on all of the grassy areas around campus.

Best Place to Meet Guys/Girls:

Because students are drawn toward the city of San Francisco, staying on campus long enough to meet guys and girls can sometimes be more of a task than making the first move. However, those students who aren't afraid to be assertive and extroverted will have no problem meeting people at USF. The most popular ways are through clubs and organizations, chatting up people sitting outside, or getting to know your classmates through study sessions and talking before or after class. If you'd rather meet people that do not attend USF, you should head to bars and cafés around the other universities in the city, like UCSF or SF State. If you're tired of searching the college scene for hot guys or girls, the downtown and Marina districts of San Francisco are overflowing with good-looking people.

Top Places to Find Hotties:

- Outside on the lawn on warm days
- Campus clubs and organizations
- Basketball games

Top Places to Hookup:

- Dorm rooms
- Dorm lounges
- Off-campus parties
- Between baseball field and Hayes-Healy
- Lone Mountain Courtyard

Dress Code:

At USF, and in San Francisco, anything goes. A large number of students here dress to be seen, even when going to an 8 a.m. class. There are a lot of "rich kids" on campus, which means that there are a lot of stylish, sharply-dressed students. But on the same token, there are just as many students whose clothing represents who they are and how they feel. From USF logo sweatshirts to American Eagle to hand-made clothing, everyone at USF is comfortable wearing whatever they want.

Students Speak Out On...
Guys & Girls

"The guys are okay; they're not really that hot though, and there are not too many of them. The ones that are hot are the athletes, but they can be conceited. The girls are fine, but there are too many of them."

Q "The girls are, by and large, **smart, beautiful, exotic**, and way out of my league."

Q "I've noticed **more ladies than guys on campus**, which isn't too bad, considering in San Francisco there's less competition (if you know what I mean). If you run out of options for a weekend date, there are plenty of other fine ladies at the various neighboring universities. Note: the UCSF Med-students, especially the guys, are always looking for girls."

Q "**Spending sunny days out on the grass** or joining campus clubs are great ways of not only making new friends; you can also check out the hotties at the school."

Q "The guys can be kind of cliché and the girls can be very needy 'college girls'. **Everyone is pretty trendy**, whether it's trendy-normal or trendy-in-their-own-style."

Q "The students are **as attractive as should be expected** from any West Coast college."

Q "The girls are very good. There are all different types of girls-many different personalities. You are bound to find girls that interest you. Also, most of them are **down-to-earth yet still intelligent**-which is nice to find. Plus, there is a pretty good ratio of girls-to-guys."

Q "There are **so many intelligent, sexy, hot guys on campus**, and this is balanced by the array of sexy chicks. Sometimes, however, there may be a great pressure to dress well, look good, and fit in simply because so many of the other students are so hot."

Q "**There are not enough guys here!** But you're not stuck, because there are plenty of places to run into cute people in the city. It's not fair; the girls are cuter than the guys."

Q "I think the ratio is 5:1. Guys are shady; there's maybe ten cute ones total, but **there are definitely cute girls**, especially the Hawaiians."

Q "There aren't a lot of guys that go to our school. Most girls say they wouldn't date guys from our school because they aren't hot and really don't have a lot to offer, but lucky me-I found one of the hot ones and we have been dating for two years. We met in a biological psychology class. I think **the girls here can be snobby, prissy, and catty.** A lot of them come from rich families. I think they are pretty, but not all that hot."

Q "**I can't say who is hot or not**; the answer to that question of taste differs for everyone."

Q "There are a lot of attractive guys, but **a lot of them are gay**. It is San Francisco, after all! Also, the last time I heard, the ration of women to men was 70:30-so, good luck ladies"

The College Prowler Take On...
Guys & Girls

For the most part, USF is an attractive campus with attractive people. Lots of the girls dress to impress not just the guys but everyone. Showing skin is pretty popular, even in the classroom. However, due to the weather, most people hide under large coats and sweatshirts in the winter. The guys, usually cloaked in jeans and a t-shirt, are quite friendly and approachable-sometimes more often than the girls. The girls sometimes get complaints of being cliquey or catty, but that's not the general consensus.

Students at USF often complain about the ratio of girls to guys, as well as the lack of available hotties to choose from. Much of this comes from the fact that USF is a very small school, will just fewer than 4,000 students. Fortunately, as most will agree, the number of undergraduates has nothing on the number of attractive and intriguing people on campus. Because USF is so diverse, there are lots of appealing guys and girls; the hardest part is getting to know them. Since USF is located in a very glamorous city with an abundance of beautiful people, stepping off campus for an evening is bound to yield a hottie or two.

The College Prowler™ Grade on
Guys: B-

A high grade for Guys indicates that the male population on campus is attractive, smart, friendly, and engaging, and that the school has a decent ratio of guys to girls.

The College Prowler™ Grade on
Girls: A-

A high grade for Girls not only implies that the women on campus are attractive, smart, friendly, and engaging, but also that there is a fair ratio of girls to guys.

Athletics

The Lowdown On...
Athletics

Athletic Division:
NCAA Division I

Conference:
WCC

**Number of Males
Playing Varsity Sports:**
118(4%)

Men's Varsity Sports:
Baseball
Basketball
Cross Country
Golf
Soccer
Rifle
Tennis

→

Number of Females Playing Varsity Sports:
95(2%)

Women's Varsity Sports:
Basketball
Cross Country
Golf
Soccer
Rifle
Tennis
Track
Volleyball

Club Sports:
Fencing
Volleyball
Rugby
Karate (Shotokan)
Kung Fu
Golf
Ski and Snowboard

Intramurals:
Co-ed Basketball
Flag Football
Co-ed Volleyball
Co-ed Indoor Soccer

Fields/Facilities:
Ulrich Field and Benedetti Diamond, Negoesco Stadium

School Mascot
Dons

Getting Tickets:
Tickets are available at the ticket office outside the Memorial Gym and also at the Dons Depot on the second floor of the UC. Tickets are free for students.

Most Popular Sports:
In terms of presence, the basketball, baseball, and volleyball teams enjoy the most spectators and student support, even though they are lacking compared to other sports-oriented schools. Intramural and club sports are the most popular because they are praised throughout the school as the most fun.

Overlooked Teams:

The rifle, tennis, and golf teams are all unfortunately the most overlooked because most students are unaware of their existence.

Best Place to Take a Walk:

Go to Golden Gate Park or just stroll around the city.

Gyms/Facilities:

Koret Health and Recreation Center

Koret is one of the largest workout centers in San Francisco; it caters to all USF students and faculty, as well as residents from around the city. Koret boasts a large, Olympic-sized indoor pool, basketball courts, a weight room, a martial arts room, an aerobics and dance room, racquetball courts, indoor batting cages, state of the art cardiovascular machines, locker rooms, and showers.

Memorial Gymnasium

Built in 1958 and one of the oldest gyms in the West Coast Conference, Memorial Gym houses the basketball and volleyball teams. It is also the stadium the Dons use for home games and practice. The athlete's locker rooms and coaches' offices are also located here.

Did You Know?

Before the 1950's, USF used to have a football team. In 1950, the Dons Football team was so good that nine of the players went onto the NFL. Unfortunately, the school couldn't afford to maintain the sport, so in 1951, the president of USF dropped football. The university revived the team in 1965, only to have it dropped again for good in 1971.

Athletes

> "Intramurals are pretty popular at USF. If there is a sport you enjoy, definitely try to participate in the IM. Soccer, basketball, baseball, and volleyball are also popular."

Q "I don't think the varsity sports are very big and **we really don't have a lot of school spirit**. I think one of the reasons why is because we don't have band; all great sports schools have a great band, and it really does help. I think the Intramurals have a lot of options and are above average."

Q "It's not really a sports school, though they are competitive and **you can see some good games**, as well as some big-name schools. They're pretty fun, particularly when people come out to the games. As for IM sports-they are a ton of fun! Also, after seeing other schools' IM programs, I would have to say that USF's are better than most-as far as competition is concerned, as well as the fun-factor."

Q "There's that crowd of varsity people, but I don't know many of them. **They don't really rule the school** or anything."

Q "**Varsity sports aren't huge**, but we support the Dons. Intramural sports are easy to get in and a lot of fun."

Q "Sports at USF are really popular among the athletes themselves. They have a small following, but, overall, the campus is pretty apathetic toward the teams. **The school treats the athletes like they are gods**, but then again, they also exploit them at times. If you're a volleyball or basketball player and you want to come here, be careful."

Q "Intramural soccer and basketball are pretty big. Our main varsity sport that brings in the biggest crowd is basketball, especially because **we are in Division I**."

Q "Sport life is lacking; **it's pretty pathetic** in all respects."

Q "Men's basketball is big, and so are soccer and volleyball. **A lot of people like the Intramurals**, especially because the gym is so nice."

Q "If you're going to root for any team on campus, make it the basketball team. It's the most exciting and has had the best record over the past few years. **The other teams are just sub-par**. If you're into intramurals, they are really fun-more fun than any other Dons team."

Q "Basketball is so much fun. **I'm excited about baseball season** as well, but since they haven't had any home games yet, we don't know just how fun it is! Other than that, I'm not big into any other sports, and no one else really makes a big deal out of the other ones, either."

Q "There's an undeniable apathy about sports at USF. **School spirit is practically nonexistent**. Many people do intramurals, though."

Q "USF's sport life is pathetic. The lack of a football team is just lame. To be cool, **root for local and regional teams like the Giants** or the A's or Sacramento Kings, not the Dons."

The College Prowler Take On...
Athletics

School spirit and sports at USF are a Catch-22. Because there is little school spirit, students heavily involved in the sports scene at USF are few and far between. Because there are few Dons sports fans at USF, there isn't much school spirit. Why this cycle exists is relatively unknown and generally not even thought about. Most students admit they are too busy to attend games, yet there is a huge amount of participation in the intramural sports program. USF students say that the intramural sports are more fun and entertaining, so the students are therefore more inclined to play the sport than to watch it. Also, many students abandon the school and utilize the professional teams in San Francisco and the Bay Area (such as the 49'ers, A's, Giants, Raiders, and Warriors) to entertain their sports needs.

It is rather unfortunate that sports teams at USF have such a small following. There are a fair amount of athletes with amazing potential, but aside from these athletes and their friends, the majority of people you'll see at Dons games are either alumni or fans of the opposing team. However, when a Dons team starts winning more games word spreads like wildfire creating many fair-weather fans, and the Dons fan base doubles overnight. This is usually the case with the men's basketball and the women's volleyball teams. The best thing for any newcomer to do is to check out at least one game at USF, and then decide if the whole Dons scene is your thing.

The College Prowler™ Grade on

Athletics: C+

A high grade in Athletics indicates that students have school spirit, that sports programs are respected, that games are well-attended, and that intramurals are a prominent part of student life.

Nightlife

The Lowdown On...
Nightlife

Club and Bar Prowler:
Popular Nightlife Spots!

Club Crawler:
Bubble Lounge

714 Montgomery, North Beach/Financial District

(415) 434-4204

www.bubblelounge.com

The Bubble Lounge boasts a chic, two-tiered space serving champagne, live music, and savory bites. While it is pricey, there is never a cover. Dress to be seen, and chill out on the bottom floor lounge while DJs spin and beautiful people lounge on red-velvet couches that are illuminated by candlelight. Fair warning: while the music is fun and the atmosphere gorgeous, Bubble Lounge tends to get very crowded and hot in its tiny little space.

Wednesdays: Live jazz upstairs

Friday and Saturday: DJs on bottom floor

DNA Lounge

375 Eleventh Street, SoMa

(415) 626-1409

→

www.dnalounge.com

Occupancy: 600

DNA Lounge has one of the larger dance floors in San Francisco, a city known for limited space. Things get pumping well after 11 p.m., so plan to hit this industrial/high-tech hot spot (complete with free Internet kiosks throughout the club) later on during your evening out.

Friday: Remedy (deep house and hip hop), $15-$20

Saturday: special events, check website

Ruby Skye

420 Mason, Downtown

(415) 693-0777

www.rubyskye.com

Unlike most venues, Ruby Skye stays open well after the last call at 2 a.m. and, as a result, is always extremely crowded. This club is unbelievably chic and expensive, and those who frequent Ruby Skye are dressed to impress. The dancing is awesome and features genres like Funk, Soul, R&B, Techno, Industrial, and Electronica.

Thursday: Various Concerts (see website)

Friday: Square, $20 cover

Saturday: Mixed Emotions, $20 cover (until 3 a.m.)

1751 Social Club

1751 Fulton, USF

(415) 441-1751

www.1751socialclub.com

The Social Club mixes dining, dancing, and great specials. It is only down the street from campus, on Fulton and Masonic. On the weekend, admission is charged after 10 p.m., so go early enough to eat dinner and then stay for dancing. Tuesday nights are also very popular because of the $3 pitchers of beer and late-night dining.

Friday and Saturday: Dancing-Jazz and Hip Hop

Bar Prowler:
The Bitter End

441 Clement Street, Richmond

(415) 221-9538

The Bitter End is infamous with USF students, due to the great specials and well-attended trivia contests. This bar also has an upstairs game room with pool tables, dartboards, and pinball machines. The Bitter End is very popular on weeknights with USF kids and is a short walk from campus.

Monday: All draft beers are $3

Tuesday: Trivia Tuesdays with cash prizes and awards for best team name and best limerick

Cha Cha Cha

1801 Haight St

(415) 386-7670

http://chachacha.citysearch.com/?cslink=

Cha Cha Cha is a popular Haight Street haunt, crowded every night of the week. Aside from ordering pitchers of sangria, try the calamari, but stay away from some of the other tapas. Students like to go here before clubbing.

Holy Cow

1535 Folsom, SoMa

(415) 621-6087

www.theholycow.com

Technically a bar, Holy Cow also poses as a mini-club on the weekends and is a great place to meet other USF kids, as well as members of the young SF crowd. DJs vary the music, from top-40 to hardcore Rap to 80s. When USF students frequent the Holy Cow, they always have a great time; it has no cover and serves up awesome Purple Hooters.

Thursday: Half-priced drinks all day

Pat O'Shea's Mad Hatter

3848 Geary Blvd

(415) 752-3148

Better known as O'Shea's, this sports bar on Geary is also popular with USF kids and is supportive of the Dons. They have dozens of TVs for plenty of sports-watching action, and O'Shea's serves up a number of microbrews and tasty fish-and-chips.

Tuesday: Ladies' Night

Wednesday: Quiz Night and live DJ music

Friday: Live music

Saturday: Live music and from 9 p.m.-12 a.m., Pilsner pints are $3 and pitchers are $10.

Other Places to Check Out:

Trader Sam's, Abbey Tavern, Last Day Saloon, Buena Vista Café, Blarney Stone, Mucky Duck, Yancy's, Slim's, Make-Out Room, 850 Cigar Bar, Café du Nord, Butter, Roccapulco, Hobson's Choice, Mad Dog in the Fog, Chances, Café Vesuvio, El Rio

Favorite Drinking Games:

Beer Pong

Card Games

Century Club

Quarters

Power Hour

Student Favorites:

- Mel's Diner
- AMC Van Ness Theater
- Trader Sam's Bar
- Abbey Tavern
- Holy Cow
- Bitter End
- North Beach
- Haight Street
- Cha Cha Cha's

Useful Resources for Nightlife:

- The Guardian
- SF Weekly
- http://sanfrancisco.citysearch.com

Primary Areas with Nightlife:

- Geary Blvd.
- SOMA (South of Market)
- Downtown
- Marina
- Castro
- Mission

Bars Close At:

2 a.m.

Cheapest Place to Get a Drink:

Mission District

Local Specialties:

Irish Coffee (invented at the Buena Vista)

Frats

See the Greek Section!

What to Do if You're Not 21:

City Nights
715 Harrison Street, SoMa (415) 339-8686
City Nights is a popular club for the eighteen-and-over crowd. Complete with five go-go cages, three bars, and multiple dance floors, City Nights is the perfect place to dance the night away to your favorite Electronica and house tunes.

330 Ritch
330 Ritch Street, SoMa (415) 541-9574
330 Ritch is a popular club that morphs itself into a different scene every night. Hosting a wide range of venues, from 60s mod to punk to upscale rhythm and blues, everyone can find their niche here.
Thursday: Popscene-Britpop beats for the eighteen-and-up crowd.

Organization Parties:

Occasionally clubs and Greek colonies will sponsor events off campus in restaurants or banquet halls. One of the most popular is the Rose Dance, put on by the Delta Sigma Pi Fraternity, which is reminiscent of a college-level prom. Also, each academic department will usually throw parties for majors at the beginning and end of each semester, so check with your respective department for more information so you can enjoy the free food!

Students Speak Out On...
Nightlife

"Parties on campus are pretty limited to dorm drinking, which is quite abundant. There are plenty of bars and clubs a short distance away, though."

Q "There are **parties all around**, so, if you like to party, it's not hard to find a place."

Q "Not a whole lot of parties are held on campus, unless you count drinking with your friends in your dorm. Bars and clubs off campus are cool but can get expensive. (Here's a tip: **drink before you go out!**) Good spots include Holy Cow, Tunnel Top, Bamboola Lounge, Trader Sam's, Matrix, Last Day Saloon, Kennedy's, Left at Albuquerque, Café du Nord, and Sake Lab."

Q "**The off-campus parties are lousy**. Good bars are a substantial distance from campus. Buena Vista Cafe is fun for old-school San Francisco drinks."

Q "This school really doesn't throw a lot of parties. The bars and clubs are cool. To relax and unwind, I like the Bitter End on Clement or even Tommy's on Van Ness. For some fun mixed drinks, I like Trader Sam's. They have **a bar for every kind of person**, but my absolute favorite is Jazz at Pearl's, where there is romantic candlelight and incredible jazz music. You can find this awesome place in North Beach."

Q "There are parties thrown on occasion, but they are certainly **not like the typical college party**. You have to search for them because most of them are off campus."

"There are not too many parties on the USF campus itself, but the city has a pretty exciting night life. There are frequent parties off campus and **many good bars and clubs to go to**."

"You probably should go all over the city, because you can, since **the bars by campus aren't that grea**t. Haight Street has cool places about six blocks away. Cha Cha Cha is a really fun sort of Caribbean place. There are also a lot of house parties. The College Players throw good cast parties and bonfires, and they're nice to freshmen."

"USF holds parties every semester. **San Francisco has so many great clubs and bars**. Ruby Skye gets my nomination for best club; it has a very nice interior and plays great trance and deep-house music. Others are DNA Lounge, Holy Cow, Envy, Whisper, Mezzanine, and a lot of Irish pubs. The list goes on and on."

"There aren't really a lot of parties on campus that I know of, other than mostly a few people just hanging out. There are some good bars, depending on what you like. Yancy's Saloon on Irving is **a really cool bar**. For clubs, you could go to Union Street or you could go to bars on Geary."

"The bars are happening on the weekends, and weekend parties rage from time-to-time. **There's always a place to chill** around campus or off campus. As for the bar and club scene, there are hundreds in the city and you can pick which one to go to, depending on your mood. The Social Club is hot on the weekends and filled with USF kids."

"Parties don't really exist on campus, and off-campus ones usually get broken up. Bars on Haight and in the Mission are **always fun and sometimes affordabl**e."

Q "The parties and bars in the neighborhood are lack-luster at best. Needless to say, **the Greek scene is a joke**. For a good time, plan on heading downtown. North Beach-San Francisco's spin on Little Italy-bustles after dark with Old World cafés, trendy pubs, a flamenco bar, hip-hop dance spots, and gentlemen's clubs. Performances by psychedelic Brazilian popsters like 'Bat Macuma' and the occasional appearance of the traveling French Sixties rave 'Bardot-a-Gogo' attest to the Bay Area's eclectic entertainment options. Those with a taste for salsa dancing should head over to the Mission District's Roccapulco, where the weekends are always sizzling."

The College Prowler Take On...
Nightlife

In San Francisco, you can find anything that interests you, and as a result, the nightlife is jam-packed with action. Most students at USF enjoy the bar scene more than the club scene, though that is not to say many people don't enjoy both. On any given night, USF students frequent bars all over the city, particularly on Geary Blvd. and on Haight Street. But if you're not into the drinking scene, going out to the movies or to dinner at one of San Francisco's amazing restaurants are high on the list of fun things to do. There are also millions of venues for live music around the city, and they often cater to the under-twenty-one crowd.

Because taking advantage of all the city has to offer can take a toll on the wallet, students often opt to drink in their dorm rooms before going out instead of drinking at the bars. If parties with fellow college students are more your scene, you'll be rather disappointed at USF. While they do exist, parties are almost always off campus and not so easy to find. Perhaps by joining Greek life, or by making friends with those who are already involved with it, you may catch a better glimpse of the off-campus parties. This is not to say that parties off campus aren't fun, it's just that they are not really emphasized at USF.

The College Prowler™ Grade on

Nightlife: A-

A high grade in Nightlife indicates that there are many bars and clubs in the area that are easily accessible and affordable. Other determining factors include the number of options for the under-21 crowd and the prevalence of house parties.

Greek Life

The Lowdown On...
Greek Life

Number of Fraternities:
14

Percent of Undergrad Men in Fraternities:
3%

Number of Sororities:
4

Percent of Undergrad Women in Sororities:
1%

Fraternities on Campus:

Alpha Phi Omega

Alpha Sigma Nu

Beta Alpha Psi

Delta Lambda Phi Interest Group

Delta Sigma Pi

Omicron Theta Chi

Psi Chi

Sigma Alpha Epsilon

Theta Alpha Kappa

Tri-Beta (Beta Beta Beta) Biological Honor Society

Sororities on Campus:

Delta Zeta

Lambda Sigma Gamma

Omicron Theta Chi

Tri-Gamma (Gamma Gamma Gamma) Nursing Sorority

Other Greek Organizations

Greek Council

Multicultural Colonies:

Alpha Epsilon Pi

Chi Rho Omicron

Chi Upsilon Zeta

Did You Know?

The Greek Council put on a mock-American Idol competition, featuring up-and-coming singers from all of the different Greek colonies.

Students Speak Out On...
Greek Life

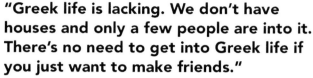

"Greek life is lacking. We don't have houses and only a few people are into it. There's no need to get into Greek life if you just want to make friends."

Q "No, **Greek life doesn't dominate the social scene**. There's only one social frat and one sorority or something low like that, so if you want it, you can have it, but you won't have much company."

Q "Greek life at USF is **not your traditional Greek life**. What we have are more like social clubs, meant for networking and service. So don't expect a bunch of keg parties or anything resembling Animal House."

Q "The Greek scene does not dominate at all! **I rarely hear of anything Greek happening**, unless I know someone in it and they happen to mention a meeting or two."

Q "There is **no Greek life**."

Q "Um, I'm not sure about Greek life. I **didn't even know there was Greek life here**."

Q "It is not dominant at all, unless you decide you want it to be, I guess. You will **not have a problem being social without associating with Greek life**, if you don't want to, which is nice. That way, you can make the choice and do what you want to do."

Q "Greek life is **virtually nonexistent**-thank God."

The College Prowler Take On...
Greek Life

While USF seems to have many Greek colonies, the majority of the fraternities and sororities on campus are service-based and/or academic-oriented. The social ones are often affiliated with a particular culture or special interest, with just one fraternity and one sorority known around campus to be purely based upon friendship and social life. There is no pressure to join, and as a result, the lack of interest shows. Most USF students are unaware and oblivious, if not entirely apathetic to Greek life. There are no designated houses on or around campus, and the majority of the Greek presence is limited to random sweatshirts with Greek letters.

Despite its low-profile presence, Greek life is involved with some campus events, such as Homecoming, the annual Greek Games, Thanksgiving Potluck, Christmas Clothing Drive, and various socials and mixers. Lately, with the Greek Council focusing on promoting more of a campus presence, some colonies are bringing their goals and interests front and center, particularly with the recent all-night teeter-totter for charity event and USF American Idol competitions. Most students said the Greek scene here at USF was virtually non-existent, which means that you will not be suffocated, like at some other schools-with pledges running around doing all sorts of crazy things. However, if Greek life is for you, then you still have the opportunity to participate.

The College Prowler™ Grade on
Greek Life: D+

A good grade means that Greek life has a highly-visible role on campus. The poorer the grade, the less prominent the Greek scene..

Drug Scene

The Lowdown On...
Drug Scene

Most Prevalent Drugs on Campus:
Alcohol

Marijuana

Cocaine

Ecstasy

Drug Counseling Programs:
USF Counseling Center, Basement Gillson Hall

Phone: (415) 422-6352

Services: The USF Counseling Center offers alcohol assessment services, short-term counseling, educational programming for groups and organizations, and provides informative alcohol-related films and literature.

C.H.O.I.C.E.S. (Choosing Healthy Options in Community Environments)

Phone: (415) 422-6702

Services: This is a group discussion session which covers the components of responsible use, legal issues, and the physiological and psychological effects of drug use and misuse. C.H.O.I.C.E.S. is an educational program for students who have violated the USF drug-free policy; it's geared toward social drinkers, not problem drinkers.

Prevention Programs, UC Third Floor

Phone: (415) 422-6702

Services: This is preventative educational programming for groups and organizations; they also have alcohol-related films and literature.

Health Services, St. Mary's Hospital

Phone: (415) 750-4980

Services: At the hospital, you can get an alcohol dependency assessment and an evaluation of alcohol on your physical well-being.

Students in Sobriety Group

Phone: (415) 422-6352

Services: This is a group counseling and discussion peer support group. Alcoholics Anonymous meetings are held weekly.

Helpline: Bay Area Resources

Phone: (415) 772-4357

Services: This telephone service offers advice and can refer callers to specific organizations that can help with their needs and/or problems.

Students Speak Out On...
Drug Scene

{ **"I have never had an experience with drugs on campus, and I have never been offered drugs. I do think, though, a lot of that has to do with the people I surround myself with."**

Q "When I lived in Phelan, **I smelled weed coming out of the vents all the time**. I also knew of a girl down the hall who did cocaine. I suppose that's normal for universities, but if you absolutely can't stand the smell of weed or the thought of being around drugs, perhaps the dorms aren't for you."

Q "I guess it's because we're in the city; you can get drugs if you want them. **People smoke in the dorms a bunch**."

Q "Drugs are basically a background presence. If you want them, you could probably get them pretty easily. However, **there isn't any pressure to take them**, and no one is standing on the corner forcing you to ingest anything. It's not a big issue unless you want it to be."

Q "There is **plenty of weed** and a good amount of other fashion drugs, which can be easily obtained in a liberal/ hippy city like SF."

Q "Students with a monkey on their backs can conveniently head off to nearby Haight Street to get their kicks. Corner deals provide even the most clean-cut junkie with the perfect fix. **Lots of drugs in the Bay Area**, you know."

Q "**I never really did any drugs**, so I haven't been around the scene."

Q "There are quite a few regular potheads. I'm assuming **a good number of people also use coke**, because a lot of students here come from major money."

Q "On campus there is **rampant weed-smoking**-almost everyone does at least a little. Occasionally, you'll encounter a few more serious drugs, but nothing too abnormal."

Q "I'm guessing it is **just like in any other universities**."

Q "It depends on who you hang out with, just like anywhere else. There are **crowds that are heavily into everything**, one drug, or just heavily into drinking. There are people that are even strictly sober. Pick the one that fits you best."

Q "Drugs are everywhere, but it's your choice if you want to get into it. From what I've seen, it's **not really pushed on you**."

The College Prowler Take On...
Drug Scene

In accordance with Jesuit principles and morals, USF has a drug-free policy, which means that every student has the right to a safe, drug-free environment. If you are caught doing drugs on campus, Public Safety officers are called and immediate disciplinary action is taken. While the consequences are tough, anyone who has ever lived in the dorms will tell you that weed is a popular drug at USF and smelling it in the halls is not uncommon.

The good news is that at USF, the drug scene is not terribly predominant, and few students ever feel pressured into taking drugs. According to the Progressive Party, a group on campus that specializes in substance abuse support for students, the perceived amount of substance abuse at USF is much higher than the actual amount. For example, the perceived percentage of students who drink three times a week or more is sixty percent, whereas the actual percentage is only nineteen percent. Also, the perceived percentage of students who smoke marijuana three or more times a week is twenty-six percent, while the actual percentage is six percent. Like any school, there are students who drink and do drugs, but at USF, substance abuse is not an immediate threat. If you don't want to get involved with drugs, you probably will never encounter them. Even if you do encounter them, no one is going to force you to take drugs if you don't want to.

The College Prowler™ Grade on

Drug Scene: B-

A good grade means that drugs are not a highly-visible threat on campus. The poorer the grade, the more prominent the drug scene.

Campus Strictness

The Lowdown On...
Campus Strictness

What Are You Most Likely to Get Caught Doing on Campus?

- Drinking underage
- Parking illegally
- Making too much noise in your dorm
- Having candles and incense in your dorm
- Running stop signs
- Graffiti or vandalism
- Doing drugs in the dorms
- Smoking closer than thirty feet to any building entrance
- Cell phones ringing in class

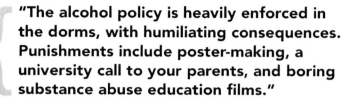

Students Speak Out On...
Campus Strictness

"The alcohol policy is heavily enforced in the dorms, with humiliating consequences. Punishments include poster-making, a university call to your parents, and boring substance abuse education films."

Q "You **don't want to get caught**, but on the other hand, I never have."

Q "There are all these threats when you first move into the dorms about not drinking, not having candles or incense in your room, not coming to the dorms drunk, etc. I remember going to a floor meeting about these issues, hung over, having just broken all of those rules within a twenty-four-hour period. Basically, **no one is going to catch you** unless you're being stupid and obvious about it."

Q "Dorm policy is **very strict** with drugs and alcohol."

Q "Basically, if you stay in control, you won't have a problem. I came as a transfer student, and I've only lived in an environment where drinking was allowed (since everyone was of age), and the outcome of that is pretty self-explanatory. **Life in Loyola Village is pretty relaxed** because of that, so it's lots of fun. There will be instances when you're going to be rushed by the cops, but I suppose that's a reality for college kids. As long as people aren't puking all over the sidewalks or screaming at strangers, and as long as they have some sort of control over themselves, there's nothing to worry about."

Q "I think **they can be pretty strict** if you get caught."

Q "They mostly get involved when things get out of hand or too loud. **They are not overly-intrusive**, which is good. At the same time, they're just trying to do their job, which sometimes might be contrary to a student's goals."

Q "It is very strict. **You'll have massive drama** to deal with if you're caught."

Q "The school is pretty laid back, as one can expect from a California university. **Don't let the Catholic front fool you**; it's pretty open and liberal. There is a no-drug policy on campus, but I have friends who've gotten away with some pretty crazy things and have still managed to keep a level head."

Q "I find it to be pretty strict, but if they don't see it, **they can't catch it**."

Q "**The campus police do what they can**, but they aren't really strict, unless you're a repeat offender. The people who think the campus police are strict are usually the RAs because they're around them all the time, but RAs can't catch everything."

Q "They can be pretty strict and unwavering. I once got caught just having a bottle of alcohol in my room, un-opened. They took it away, even though it was decorative, and **made me go to counseling**. It's best not to leave any alcohol paraphernalia in view."

The College Prowler Take On...
Campus Strictness

Most students at USF are divided over how strict the campus is, particularly in regards to alcohol in the dorms. While most people claim to get away with it, those who are caught face harsh penalties, some of which include attending substance abuse meetings, counseling, and university probation. If a student is caught doing drugs, Public Safety is immediately called, and that is embarrassing enough in itself to not do drugs on campus.

Resident Advisors live on every floor in every residence hall, and they are the ones who catch people most of the time. They are also the first authority figure for campus residents. Whether it's being too loud and disrupting neighbors, having incense or candles, or using an illegal substance, Resident Advisors typically catch offenders and subsequently have to report them to higher authorities. As college students themselves, Resident Advisors can often be as guilty as anyone else can. The most important thing to remember is that if you keep your misconduct to yourself, you won't get caught. Don't come into the dorms so drunk you can't walk, don't blast your music, and hide your candles or incense and the Resident Advisor on duty won't have to write you up.

The College Prowler™ Grade on

Campus
Strictness: C

A high Campus Strictness grade implies an overall lenient atmosphere; police and RAs are fairly tolerant, and the administration's rules are flexible.

Parking

The Lowdown On...
Parking

USF Parking Services:
(415) 422-4222

parking@usfca.edu

http://www.usfca.edu/public_
safety/parking/index.html

Student Parking Lot?
No

Freshman Allowed to Park?
Freshmen are not allowed to purchase a permit for a lot or garage; however they may park freely on the streets.

Approximate Parking Permit Cost:
Daily $6, Full-Time Semester $240, Part-Time Semester $145

Parking Permits:

Permits are issued via lottery and only 175 are issued to students.

No on-campus students may apply for permits.

Applications for the lottery are available the prior semester.

Common Parking Tickets:

Expired Meter: $35
No Parking Zone: $50
Handicapped Zone: $275
Fire Lane: $25

Best Places to Find a Parking Spot:

There are no places to find a good parking spot, let alone any old parking spot.

Good Luck Getting a Parking Spot Here:

Anywhere in San Francisco!

Students Speak Out On...
Parking

"Just in case you haven't watched enough movies or television, San Francisco is very hilly. Good breaks are vital, especially when trying to squeeze into parking spaces facing uphill or downhill."

Q "Parking is horrible. Sometimes it may take **half an hour to find a spot,** and even then, you'd have to move your car in two hours' time or the DPT will 'reward' you with a ticket. You can park on Lone Mountain for six dollars, but even that parking lot has limited spaces. USF has very few all-day parking spots available and it really angers me. How can you possibly move your car to another spot without getting a ticket when you have a three-hour class?."

Q "It's kind of a pain-you have to **watch out for street cleaning**, and you can't park on campus without a permit."

Q "On-campus parking is available, but you should **be prepared to pay high university prices** for permits. If you do bring a car-driver, be warned: smaller cars have a better advantage for finding parking because tight spaces seem to abound in the city. Also, when going out, it's best to take a cab or find a place with a valet, such as Bocce Café in North Beach."

Q "Parking is really bad-**don't bring a car!**"

Q "There is hardly any parking available on campus. People mostly park in the streets because **it costs too much for a parking permit**. With many people in the streets, it can cause problems trying to find a spot. For the most part, I would suggest not bringing a car, if at all possible."

Q "It is hard to park, **like on all campuses.**"

Q "Parking is not as hard as some people think, but it's not easy. **Be prepared for a lot of tickets**. Also watch out for parking in residential neighborhoods because, if your car is barely covering somebody's driveway, they can (and often do) tow you. That ends up costing you $200 to get your car back."

Q "It's not easy to park on campus, but if you're willing to pay **$280 a semester** for it, then yeah, it's easy."

Q "Parking is **not easy** because you are in San Francisco."

Q "It is difficult to park, and not to mention expensive. **We need more parking structures** and permits because it's so difficult to find parking."

Q "I like to park off campus, since school lot fees are so expensive and all. **Neighborhood spots fill up fast**, and finding a good parking location before class can some-times be impossible. The next thing you know, you're late to class."

The College Prowler Take On...
Parking

As anyone with a car will tell you, parking can be your worst nightmare around USF, as well as anywhere in the city. While USF recognizes this problem, currently there is nothing being done about it. The university has two designated parking complexes-Hayes-Healy and Koret, as well as a handful of small parking lots around main campus and on Lone Mountain. Those lots, though, are strictly parking areas are for faculty or USF vehicles, leaving less than 200 available spots for students with permits, not to mention the high price of those permits. Also, freshmen and sophomores living on campus are not allowed to purchase a permit. Most students recommended not even bringing a car to USF unless it's absolutely necessary.

If you bring a car to school and reside on campus, or even if you don't live in the dorms, there are still some places to park-mainly the streets surrounding the campus. Be careful, though, because most of those spots are designated two-hour parking only. Also, around class time, you will find at least ten to twenty other students looking for the same spots that aren't there. Plan to start looking for a spot at least thirty minutes before your class starts. Remember: if you do park in a residential neighborhood, don't let your car block any driveway, even by just a half-inch. Some of the residents will not hesitate to have your car towed while you're in class.

The College Prowler™ Grade on

Parking: D-

A high grade in this section indicates that parking is both available and affordable, and that parking enforcement isn't overly severe.

The Lowdown On...
Transportation

Ways to Get Around Town
On Campus
USF Shuttle Service, Monday-Thursday 7:15 a.m.-11 p.m., Friday 7:15 a.m.-5 p.m.
(415) 422-4222
USF Escort, by request (415) 422-4222

Public Transportation:
San Francisco Municipal Railway (MUNI), (415) 673-MUNI. Schedules are available at the University Center Information Desk or from www.sfmuni.com.

Taxi Cabs
Black & White Checker Cabs Inc.
(415) 285-3800
Diamond Cab Co.
(415) 781-1138
Pacific Cab Co.
(415) 986-7220
Yellow Cab Co. Operative
(415) 626-2345

→

Car Rentals

Alamo
local: (415) 701-7400
national: (800) 327-9633
www.alamo.com
Avis
local: (415) 957-9998
national: (800) 831-2847
www.avis.com
Budget
local: (415) 775-6607
national: (800) 527-0700
www.budget.com
Dollar
national: (800) 800-4000
www.dollar.com
Enterprise
local: (415) 546-6777
national: (800) 736-8222
www.enterprise.com
Hertz
local: (415) 387-0136
national: (800) 654-3131
www.hertz.com
National
local: (415) 474-5300
national: (800) 227-7368
www.nationalcar.com
Thrifty
local: (415) 399-3990
national: (800) 847-4389
www.thrifty.com

Best Ways to Get Around Town:

Busses-they cover the entire city and are free with your student MUNI pass.

Walking-San Francisco is beautiful on foot, as long as the weather is welcoming.

Taxi Cabs-After those late nights out drinking and dancing, calling a cab is never a bad idea.

Classic Streetcars and Cable Cars-Even if you don't use these often as your primary mode of transportation, it still can be fun and interesting to ride on what some would say is a part of San Francisco history.

Ways to Get Out of Town:

Airlines Serving San Francisco:
Air Canada
(888) 247-2262
www.aircanada.com
Alaska Airlines
(800) 252-7522
www.alaskaair.com
America West Airlines
(800) 327-7810
www.americawest.com
American Airlines
(800) 433-7300
www.americanairlines.com
Continental
(800) 523-3273
www.continental.com
Delta
(800) 221-1212
www.delta-air.com
Frontier Airlines
(800) 432-1359

www.frontierairlines.com

Hawaiian Airlines

(800) 882-8811

www.hawaiianair.com

Midwest Airlines

(800) 452-2022

www.midwestairlines.com

Northwest

(800) 225-2525

www.nwa.com

United

(800) 241-6522

www.united.com

US Airways

(800) 428-4322

www.usairways.com

Airport:

San Francisco International Airport, (650) 821-7275

SFO is eleven miles and approximately twenty minutes driving time from campus.

How to get there:

A door-to-door van ride to the airport is the most convenient way. Shuttles cost anywhere from $11 to $20.

Airport Shuttle, (415) 398-9090

American Airporter Shuttle Inc., (415) 923-6920

M & M Luxury Shuttle, (415) 552-3200

Super Shuttle, (415) 558-8500

Also, you can take MUNI #5 Fulton bus downtown and exit on Market at Civic Center. From there, you can take the BART outbound to the airport. The MUNI ride is free with a student pass and the BART ride costs $3-$5. This is probably the most cost-efficient mode of transporting yourself to the airport.

A Cab Ride to the Airport Costs:

$30

Greyhound Bus Lines

The Greyhound Trailways Bus Terminal is in downtown San Francisco, approximately six miles from campus. For schedule information, call (800) 231-2222 or visit www.greyhound.com.

San Francisco Greyhound Bus Lines

425 Mission St # 3

San Francisco, CA 94105

(415) 495-1569

Amtrak

The closest Amtrak Train Station is in Oakland, which is across the bay and approximately sixteen miles from campus. For schedule information, call (800) 872-7245 or visit www.amtrak.com.

Oakland Amtrak Train Station
245 2nd Street
Oakland, CA 94607
(510) 238-4320

Travel Agents

Travel Agents

Clement Travel Agency, located on the second floor of the University Center, (415) 422-6137

Campus Travel, 441 Irving St # 447, Inner Sunset, (415) 753-1400

Clement Travel Svc Inc., 14 Clement St, Richmond, (415) 386-2535

Students Speak Out On...
Transportation

> "Transportation is great. Make sure you use the trip planner option on www.sfmuni.com; it will save you so much time."

"It's awesome. Get a map that shows the bus routes, and **you can get to anywhere from anywhere**. It took me two years to get it down, but now I'm set. There is a bunch of bus lines right around campus that go downtown and across town, too."

"**Very convenient**, but it gets old without a car; especially when hauling home groceries."

"Transportation in San Francisco is very convenient. **I did not have a car all four years here**, and I've never had any issues with getting anywhere. It would be quite nice to have a car, but it's not a necessity at all. Not to mention that the parking tickets (which are inevitable) make you think twice."

"Every USF student can get a MUNI sticker pass on their ID card, so take advantage of it and see San Francisco! **The transportation system is phenomenal**."

"Very convenient! Besides the fact that buses run pretty regularly, **San Francisco is not that big of a town**-so it's pretty easy to get from one place to another."

"After your first semester, **you learn how to make the buses, trains, and cabs convenient**. It's mostly about learning the routes and the reliability of each route."

Q "Pretty convenient; **buses come every fifteen minutes**, usually."

Q "San Francisco's public transportation system, called the MUNI, can get you just about anywhere on the Peninsula. The **student bus pass included in tuition gets you unlimited access to any bus, streetcar, and cable car** in town-so take advantage and enjoy! BART stations along Market Street are great for East Bay escapes like Berkeley, Lake Merrit, or the Oakland Coliseum."

Q "**Free bus rides are perfect**. Having a car is a bit of a pain, but the Geary bus and a pair of good shoes can make up for it."

Q "Pretty convenient. **We have the MUNI buses**, **BART**, and the **Caltrain**."

The College Prowler Take On...
Transportation

If you've never been to San Francisco, you'll soon realize that parking is not only expensive but virtually impossible. Not to mention the facts that most streets are narrow, uphill, and two-lanes (and that's if you're lucky and it's not a one-way). In order to get around with ease, MUNI is your only answer. The San Francisco Municipal Railway is actually one of the most efficient and reliable transit systems in the United States, though the busses are known to frequently run off schedule. The good news is that MUNI claims they are on time twenty-five percent more often than in 2000.

MUNI busses run up and down almost every street you'd want to go, or close enough to anywhere you'd want to go-so if you are relying on a bus to get you from point A to point B, you won't have much walking to do at all. There are also metro-style cars that run from downtown to the outer areas of the city, old fashioned streetcars (the actual ones used in the early Twentieth century, from San Francisco to Philadelphia to Milan), and of course the infamous trolley cars that even native San Franciscans can't resist from time-to-time. Typically, a one-way ride costs $1.25, but as a student of USF, you'll receive a MUNI Pass that allows you unlimited rides on all MUNI transit systems. This MUNI Pass is free because the cost is included in every student's tuition. There is a reason why almost every SFU student relies on MUNI; it's the very best and most convenient way around town and the Bay Area.

The College Prowler™ Grade on

Transportation: A-

A high grade for Transportation indicates that campus buses, public buses, cabs, and rental cars are readily-available and affordable. Other determining factors include proximity to an airport and the necessity of transportation.

Weather

The Lowdown On...
Weather

Average Temperature
Fall: 52°F
Winter: 44°F
Spring: 49°F
Summer: 55°F

Average Precipitation
Fall: 1.24 in.
Winter: 3.78in.
Spring: 1.61in.
Summer: 0.21 in

"Bring everything! You can never guess what the weather will be like. It does not snow here, that's the only thing I can tell you. But bring clothes for every other possible climate change."

Q "When you first come to school in the fall, **expect to be in shorts until around Halloween**. Then it gets foggy, cold, and rainy well past winter break. If you're lucky, by spring break you'll get a beach weekend in. I haven't experienced the city in May though, but spring is a beautiful time of year here. Basically, fall and spring are the best and the summer and winter are almost the same."

Q "The weather is **foggy, rainy, and cold** but it lightens up on and off throughout the year."

Q "The weather changes all the time, but it's mostly cool. Bring layers, because **you never know when the fog will start rolling in** or when it might start raining. Yes, it is California, but it is Northern California."

Q "The weather is **awesome in the fall**-that's the real summer. Winter is foggy and rainy. Layers, layers, layers."

Q "San Francisco is pretty chilly and windy-very **light-jacket weather all the time**. Bring a jacket and plenty of sweatshirts."

Q "Bring stuff you can layer because one part of campus can be cold and foggy while another is sunny and warm. You could leave the house dressed for a sunny day and come back in two hours freezing (or vice versa). **Layering is key!**"

Q "**The weather is pretty mild**. You should bring a sweatshirt, jeans, flip-flops, and t-shirts."

Q "The weather is constantly changing, though **it never really gets extremely cold or extremely hot**. Depending on what you are used to, jeans and a sweatshirt are generally good enough. Make sure that you have a medium-weight coat, particularly for wind and rain."

Q "It is basically **chilly and cold all year round** in San Francisco, except for spring and summer. Even then, although the weather is hot, the winds may still be a little chilly for some."

Q "**Weather patterns vary from day-to-day** and, surprisingly, hour-to-hour. Wear layers-you never know when a fog drift might roll in or out. Comfortable shoes are suggested for the City's hilly terrain, not to mention climbing up Lone Mountain. A swimsuit is perfect for the Koret pool or sunny-day tanning in the warm California sun."

The College Prowler Take On...
Weather

When Mark Twain said, "The coldest winter I have ever known was the summer I spent in San Francisco," he was absolutely correct. The summer and winter are practically indistinguishable, with chilling winds and lots of fog. However, the winter also has quite a bit of rain (never snow), which lasts from November to February. You can't rely on the weather here, unless you rely on it being unpredictable. In the midst of a freezing summer, San Francisco can reach temperatures as high as a hundred degrees (with no air conditioning). The best advice is to always wear layers, because while most days are mild, the temperature can change in an instant.

Look forward to lots of sunny, clear days during the beginning of the fall semester. (Shorts and capri pants are awesome for this weather.) During this weather, the campus is crowded with scantily clad students sunning themselves on every grassy patch of the campus. In the summer, be sure to have a sweater handy, and as for the rest of the year, wear layers, and you'll never be unprepared.

The College Prowler™ Grade on

Weather: A-

A high Weather grade designates that temperatures are mild and rarely reach extremes, that the campus tends to be sunny rather than rainy, and that weather is fairly consistent rather than unpredictable.

Report Card Summary

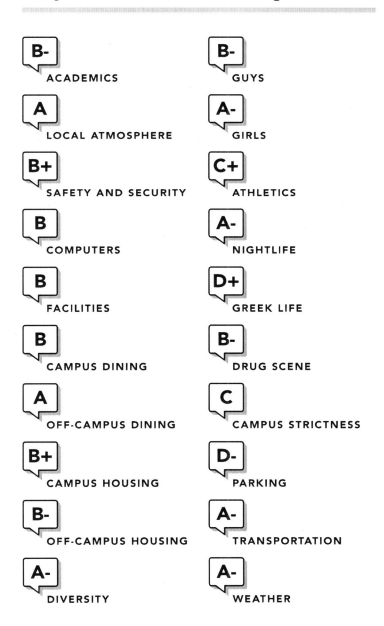

B-
ACADEMICS

A
LOCAL ATMOSPHERE

B+
SAFETY AND SECURITY

B
COMPUTERS

B
FACILITIES

B
CAMPUS DINING

A
OFF-CAMPUS DINING

B+
CAMPUS HOUSING

B-
OFF-CAMPUS HOUSING

A-
DIVERSITY

B-
GUYS

A-
GIRLS

C+
ATHLETICS

A-
NIGHTLIFE

D+
GREEK LIFE

B-
DRUG SCENE

C
CAMPUS STRICTNESS

D-
PARKING

A-
TRANSPORTATION

A-
WEATHER

Overall Experience

Students Speak Out On...
Overall Experience

"I like USF, and I'm not planning on trans-ferring. However, it is definitely a financial burden, especially because they raise the tuition almost every other year."

Q "I love this city. **The school has been pretty great**. Some of my professors are really wonderful and have helped me a lot. I'm planning on staying in San Francisco, and I'm glad I had time in college to get to know the city a little. I feel like I'm at home here now (after four years) and that I've gained some skills."

Q "I love the school because the people are great, but I think **the requirements for graduation need to be revised**, especially for transfer students. The requirements now make it harder to graduate on time."

Q "I've had a great time at USF. The school is good, the people are great, and the city is phenomenal. I'm **glad I decided to go here** as opposed to anywhere else, especially Milwaukee, because I was really close to going to Marquette."

Q "I could not have made a better choice for a university. My four years here are almost up, and I can definitely say **it's been a fun ride**. Oh yeah, and the education is great, too!"

Q "I loved my experience at USF, but my only regret is that I didn't go here all four years. **Since I transferred, I felt left out** and it was harder to make friends when everyone seemed to already have their friends. The only thing I don't like about it is how expensive it is."

Q "Overall, I would say that it has been a very good time at USF, with **a good diversity of experiences**. Going to college in a big city is something I would recommend, particularly if you want to do things apart from the school at times. The education is good, just try to find something you like to do and learn about. Personally, I am glad I am here, because I think that at a bigger school, I may have been lost in the crowd a bit, whereas here, you can create relationships both with students and professors, which is helpful."

Q "My overall experience is good. **I wish I could have been in Berkeley**, but the cultural and social experience of living in San Francisco is unbelievable."

Q "I am so unbelievably glad I transferred here. **The tuition is extremely high**, but part of that can be expected from a city like San Francisco. I love this school, though, and the city. The size is small, but not so small you can't meet anyone new. I also enjoy the faculty and the aesthetics of the campus. It's absolutely beautiful! Especially Saint Ignatius Church, when it's lit up at night and shrouded in fog, it's absolutely beautiful. I'm also glad USF is making so many renovations because they were long overdue. The renovations will make the school even better for years to come."

Q "Overall, I am mostly pleased with USF. The faculty has been very supportive of my lifestyle choices. **The religious presence was a bit awkward** at first and it might continue to be for students not used to it, but the general outlook of the school is secular and tolerant."

Q "**I couldn't be happier** anywhere but good old San Francisco."

Q "Overall, my experience at USF has been favorable and stimulating. Comparatively, **it might not be the best school for your resume**, but I feel like I'm getting pretty good preparation for grad school. I've had a lot of friends who graduated ahead of me get into some really good schools. Just keep in mind, this isn't Harvard. I was able to do everything at the last minute and still get high honors. I'm still glad I went here because I love the small departments. (They pay attention to all your academic needs.). Getting to know all of my peers and the city of San Francisco has made all the difference."

Q "So far, so good. I've had a great time here both academically and socially. Somehow I feel like I was meant to be here. Now that it's time to graduate, **I feel really sad about leaving USF**. I've grown so much as a person and as a writer here."

Q "USF is a great school. If you are looking for a school that is gorgeous and relatively small, then this is the school for you. There are **plenty of things to keep you busy** while you enjoy the intellectual challenges and exotic releases that a city like San Francisco has to offer!"

The College Prowler Take On...
Overall Experience

Most students will tell you that the best thing about USF is the city of San Francisco. Granted, the city provides an amazing backdrop, but the school itself is also very fascinating and, in some ways, is reflective of the city. Like San Francisco, USF is quite old, with a rich history and a positive outlook on the future. You'll find building after building being renovated, in order to keep up with the times and the demands of the students. You will also find students with strong morals, dedicated to service and justice, and most importantly, a university that supports them. Also like the city it resides in, USF is incredibly diverse and tolerant. Coming here, you will meet people from all over the world, of all ethnicities, religions, and cultures. Taking advantage of these amazing opportunities, both inside and outside of the classroom, can mold any student into a conscious, cultured, and well-grounded individual.

USF gives its students the opportunity to enjoy both the intimacy of a small college experience and life in the big city. When the campus feels too consuming or school work becomes too demanding, San Francisco provides an amazing release. Students here take advantage of the different cultures, views, restaurants, museums, and nightlife the city has to offer. In the end, USF students find nothing better than this stunning combination of an amazing university and the city of San Francisco.

The Inside Scoop

The Lowdown On...
The Inside Scoop

USF Slang:

Know the slang, know the school. The following is a list of things you really need to know before coming to USF. The more of these words you know, the better off you'll be.

The UC: The University Center, located at the heart of main campus

Harney 240 or 240: Location of the Arts and Sciences Dean's office

On the Hill: On Lone Mountain

The gym: Koret Health and Recreation Center, not Memorial Gym

Dead Hour: 12:00-1:00; lunchtime, when no classes are held

Parina: Popular lounge on the third floor of the UC; also a computer lab

RA: Resident Advisor; each residence hall has at least one on each floor

→

Resident Minister: Each residence hall has at least one or two in each building; they serve as inspirational leaders and support students with whatever problems they might have

ITS: Information Technology Services; they are the people to go to with computer and network problems or questions

SI: Usually refers to Saint Ignatius church, but can also mean the Saint Ignatius Institute

World Fare: Old name for the Market Cafeteria

School Spirit

While almost every student at USF owns some article of clothing bearing the USF logo, school spirit is practically obsolete. Part of this comes from being regarded as the snobs of the city, according to the other universities in San Francisco. Another part of this comes from the city itself. While San Francisco is one of the best things about USF, it is also one of the worst. All the incentives to explore the city and hang out off campus end up dividing the students, who rarely mingle with each other unless they live in the dorms or are required to meet for a group project. Also, USF has few traditions or large-scale events that increase school spirit. Most students are enthusiastic about their respective interests, and other than that, graduation is the only time when everyone comes together to celebrate their school spirit.

Things I Wish I Knew Before Coming to USF:

If you know you'll get tired of eating the same thing, pick the smallest meal plan and eat off campus the rest of the time.

USF is a Jesuit Catholic school

Greek Life has little presence on campus

That smell in your dorm room will go away

That smell in the dorm hallway won't go away

Get to know your advisor and try to keep them throughout your entire college career

You have to take writing and public speaking, no matter what your major is

Most professors have a strict attendance policy

Tips to Succeed at USF:

Get involved with any and all clubs and organizations that interest you

Take advantage of your professor's office hours and accessibility

Use your USF Connect e-mail account, and check it often!

Attend campus lectures and Lone Mountain readings

Go to class and participate

Take advantage of the diversity and learn about a new culture

Visit museums and participate in cultural activities in the city

Use your free membership at Koret

Do not bring a car to USF

USF Urban Legends:

Lone Mountain is haunted by the ghost of a nun who killed herself after being impregnated by a priest

USF is built on top of a cemetery and not all of the bodies were moved

Students at USF are the snobs of the college scene in San Francisco, due to the high price of tuition, private status of the school, and all the rich kids that go here

Finding a Job or Internship

The Lowdown On...
Finding a Job or Internship

The Lowdown:

The Career Services Center and the university make finding an internship fairly easy for students. Most majors offer an internship course as a means of fulfilling the Service Learning aspect of the Core Curriculum. More often than not, if you like your internship and make a great impression, the employer will offer you a position by the time you graduate.

Advice:

Check out http://www.usfca.edu/career for access to the CSC internship database and links to MonsterTrak and the USF Student-Alumni Internship Exchange, or talk to the professor in charge of internships for your major. Also, the CSC will assist you in making contacts for future employment. Keep in touch with the career counselors and leave your options open.

Career Center Resources & Services:

Career Counseling
Mock Interviews
Resume Reviews and Interview Skills
Workshops on Employment-Related Topics
Career Fairs
Job and Internship Listings
On-Campus Interviews with Employers
Externships with USF Alumni Volunteers

Average Salary Information:

The University of San Francisco does not have specific salary information for its bachelor degree graduates. The Career Services Center offers data regarding the national average at http://www.usfca.edu/career/Exploration/information.html.

Accounting	$40,647
Biological Sciences/Life Sciences	$29,456
Chemical Engineering	$52,384
Civil Engineering	$41,669
Communications	$30,565
Computer Engineering	$51,343
Computer Science	$47,109
Economics/Finance	$39,438
Electrical/Electronics and Communication Engineering	$49,794
Elementary Teacher Education	$29,702

English Language and Literature/Letters	$28,786
History	$31,862
Hospitality Services Management	$27,898
Information Sciences and Systems	$38,282
Management Information Systems/ Business Data Processing	$40,556
Marketing/Marketing Mgmt.	$34,038
Mathematics	$40,512
Mechanical Engineering	$48,585
Nursing	$46,782
Political Science/Government	$31,183
Psychology	$27,786
Secondary Education	$29,264

Other sources on the web:

http://www.wageweb.com

http://www.salary.com

Firms Most Frequently Hire Graduates:

- Deloitte and Touche
- Price Waterhouse
- KPMG
- Earnst & Young
- Fairmont Hotels
- Marriott
- UCSF
- California Pacific Medical Center

Alumni

The Lowdown On...
Alumni

Website:
http://www.usfca.edu/online/
alum_giving/

Office:
USF Alumni Association
2310 Fulton Street, LMR 112
San Francisco, CA 94117-1048
(415) 422-6431 or
1-800-449-4USF
alumni@usfca.edu

Services Available:
Alumni membership at Koret
Health and Recreation Center

Access to Gleeson Library and
Geschke Center with Alumni
card

Career Development and
networking through the Career
Services Center

Lifetime e-mail address

Major Alumni Events

The Alumni Association sponsors the Homecoming basketball game and offers a pre-game microbrew tasting, a SF Giants game event, reunions, and wine tasting in Sonoma, CA. Also, there are chapters of alumni in various cities in the Bay Area and across the nation, and each respective chapter holds its own events.

USF Magazine

The USF Magazine is an automatic perk of graduating from USF, as well as from making any donation to the school. There is also an internet version of the magazine, called USF News (http://www.usfca.edu/usfnews/), which features news on all aspects of USF life.

Student Organizations

ASUSF - http://www.usfca.edu/asusf

Campus Activities Board (CAB)

College Players - http://www.asusfcollegeplayers.com

Freedom Alliance of Culturally Empowered Students (FACES)

Greek Council - http://www.usfca.edu/org/greekcouncil

International Student Association (ISA) - http://www.usfca.edu/org/isa

KDNZ

Orientation Team

The San Francisco Foghorn - http://www.usfca.edu/foghorn

Academic & Honors Societies:

African and Latino Americans Empowered Pre-Health Alliance (ALAEPHA)

American Marketing Association (AMA)

Hospitality Management Association

National Society of Collegiate Scholars

Nursing Students Association (NSA)

Pre-Dental Society

Psychology Society of Mind Klub (PSMK)

Society of Physics Students

Cultural Organizations:

Black Student Union

Brother Connection

EKTAA-Indian Student Association - http://www.usfca.edu/clubs/ektaa/

Hong Kong Student Association

Hui 'O Hawaii - http://www.usfca.edu/clubs/huiohawaii/

Kasamahan - http://www.usfca.edu/clubs/kasamahan/

Latin American Student Organization (LASO)

Sister Connection

Vietnamese Student Association

(VSA)

Y Taotao Guam

Greek Organizations:

Alpha Epsilon Pi Fraternity

Alpha Phi Omega Fraternity - www.usfca.edu/org/greekcouncil/apo.html

Alpha Sigma Nu

Beta Alpha Psi

Chi Rho Omicron Fraternity

Chi Upsilon Zeta Fraternity

Delta Lambda Phi Interest Group

Delta Sigma Pi - http://www.usfca.edu/org/dsp/

Delta Zeta Sorority - http://www.usfca.edu/org/greekcouncil/dz.html

Lambda Sigma Gamma Sorority - http://www.usfca.edu/clubs/lsgnu/

Omicron Theta Chi Fraternity - http://www.usfca.edu/org/greekcouncil/otcf.html

Omicron Theta Chi Sorority - http://www.usfca.edu/org/greekcouncil/otcs.html

Psi Chi

Sigma Alpha Epsilon Fraternity - http://www.usfca.edu/org/greekcouncil/sae.html

Theta Alpha Kappa

Tri-Beta (Beta Beta Beta) Biological Honor Society - http://www.usfca.edu/clubs/tribeta/

Tri-Gamma (Gamma Gamma Gamma) Nursing Sorority - http://www.usfca.edu/org/greekcouncil/ggg.html

Special Interest Groups:

AIESEC

Aloha Radio Productions

Association for Computing Machinery

Best Buddies

Cogito - www.usfca.edu/clubs/cogito/

Computers R Us Club

Discourse-Interdisciplinary Philosophy Journal

Economics Society

Electoral Governing Board

Envision

Equal Justice Society

Exercise and Sport Science Student Association

Graduate Business Association

Ignatians

Math Club

McLaren Student Advisory Council

Peace and Justice Coalition - www.usfca.edu/clubs/pjc/

PEACE Partners

Peers on Wellness Education and Reality (POWER)

Philosophy Club

Ray of Hope

Real Life-Intervarsity Christian Fellowship - http://www.usfca.edu/clubs/reallife/

Residence Hall Association (RHA)

Rhythm Nation

Royal Knights Chess Club

School of the Americas Watch

Society of Pre-Law

Society of Scabbard and Blade

Students & Kids Involved in Living and Learning (SKILL)

Students for Democracy

The Learning Club

The Next Movement

Those Kids With Cameras

United Third World Philosophers

University Scholars Association

Urban Arts, Indie Film Club

USF Alliance

USF Debate Club

USF Dons

USF Fencing Club

USF Lacrosse

USF Rugby Football Club (Men's & Women's)

USF Ski & Snowboard Club

USF Spirit Squad

USF Ultimate Frisbee

USF Young Democrats

Zephyr

The Best & The Worst

The Ten **BEST** Things About USF:

1. The city of San Francisco

2. The size of the school and its population

3. The aesthetics of the campus

4. Diversity

5. Quality of teaching

6. Accessibility of professors

7. MUNI Student Pass

8. Small class sizes

9. The President of the University, Stephen A. Privett, SJ

10. Ethical standards of USF education

The Ten **WORST** Things About USF:

1	Cost of tuition
2	Parking
3	Apathetic school spirit
4	Lack of events and parties on weekends
5	Four-unit system
6	Freshman and sophomore dorms
7	The 109 stairs to Lone Mountain
8	Apathy toward USF Dons sports teams
9	Older facilities
10	Unpredictable weather

Visiting USF

The Lowdown On...
Visiting USF

HOTEL INFORMATION

Downtown:
Inn at the Opera
333 Fulton Street
San Francisco, CA 94102
Reservation Line: (800) 325-2708
Direct Line: (415) 863-8400
Fax: (415) 861-0821
E-mail: carlos@silcon.com
Website: www.innattheopera.com
Special Rate: $129, includes complimentary continental buf-fet breakfast
Regular Rate: $185

Union Square:
The Powell Hotel
28 Cyril Magnin
San Francisco, CA 94102
Reservation Line: (800) 368-0700
Direct Line: (415) 398-3200
Fax: (415) 398-3654
E-mail: thepowellhotel@aol.com
Website: www.powellhotel.com

→

Special Rate: $85 or $109 includes breakfast and parking
Regular Rate: $155-$165
Booking Code: USF

Hotel Cosmo

761 Post Street
San Francisco, CA
Reservation Line: (415) 345-4154
Direct Line: (415) 673-6040
Fax: (415) 563-6739
E-mail: sales@hotelcosmo.com
Website: www.hotel-cosmo.com
Special Rate: $79
Regular Rate: $159
Booking Code: USF

Canterbury Hotel

750 Sutter Street
San Francisco, CA 94109
Reservation Line: (415) 474-6464
Direct Line: (415) 474-6464
Fax: (415) 474-0831
E-mail: vivian@canterbury-hotel.com
Website: www.canterbury-hotel.com
Special Rate: $119
Regular Rate: $119
Booking Code: 2155700

Handlery Union Square Hotel

351 Geary Street
San Francisco, CA 94102
Reservation Line: (415) 781-7800
Fax: (415) 781-0269
E-mail: reservation-sf@handlery.com
Website: www.handlery.com
Special Rate: $99
Special Package: $139 room and parking
Regular Rate: $189
Booking Code: USF Graduation

Westin St. Francis

335 Powell Street
San Francisco, CA 94102
Website: www.westin.com
Special Rate: $199
Regular Rate: $349
Booking Code: UCSF

Hilton San Francisco

333 O'Farrell Street
San Francisco, CA 94102
Reservation Line: (800) HIL-TONS
Direct Line: (415) 771-1400
Fax: (415) 771-6807
Website: www.sanfrancisco.hilton.com
Special Rate: From $129
Booking Code: USF

San Francisco Residence Club

851 California Street
San Francisco, CA 94108
Direct Line: (415) 421-2220
Fax: (415) 421-2335
E-mail: innkeeper@sfresclub.com

Website: www.sfresclub.com
Special Rate: $370-$595
weekly, $950-$1900 (4 weeks)
Regular Rate: $56-98

Daily Warwick Regis Hotel

490 Geary Street
San Francisco, CA 94102
Direct Line: (415) 928-7900
Fax: (415) 441-8788
Special Rate: $125-$135 Continental Breakfast and Buffet Lunch included
Regular Rate: $179
Booking Code: USF

Clift

495 Geary Street
San Francisco, CA 94102
Reservation Line: (800) 652-5438
Direct Line: (415) 775-4700
Fax: (415) 441-4621
Website: www.ianshragerhotels.com
Special Rate: $195-$215
Regular Rate: $325-$345
Booking Code: USF

Rate Hotel Triton

342 Grant Avenue
San Francisco, CA 94108
Reservation Line: (800) 433-6611
Direct Line: (415) 394-0500
Fax: (415) 394-0678
E-mail:

reservations@hoteltriton.com
Website: www.hoteltriton.com
Special Rate: $149
Regular Rate: $209
Booking Code: USF Graduation Rate

Campton Place Hotel

340 Stockton Street
San Francisco, CA 94108
Reservation Line: (800) 235-4300
Direct Line: (415) 781-5555
Fax: (415) 955-5536
E-mail: reserve@campton.com
Website: www.camptonplace.com
Special Rate: $225
Regular Rate: $335-$395
Booking Code: None

The Maxwell Hotel

386 Geary Street at Mason
San Francisco, CA 94102
Reservation Line: (888) 734-6299
Direct Line: (415) 986-2000
Fax: (415) 397-2447
E-mail: resmax@jdvhospitality.com
Website: www.maxwellhotel.com
Special Package: $135-$165 room + parking
Regular Rate: $165-$195 Booking Code: USF

→

The Orchard Hotel

665 Bush Street

San Francisco, CA 94108

Reservations Line: (888) 717-2881

Direct Line: (415) 362-8878

Fax: (415) 362-8088

E-mail: mnancy@theorchardhotel.com

Website: www.theorchardhotel.com

Special Rate: $239

Regular Rate: $289

Booking Code: USF

Rate Renaissance Parc 55 Hotel

55 Cyril Magnin Street

San Francisco, CA 94102

Reservations Line: (800) 650-7272

Direct Line: (415) 392-8000

Fax: (415) 421-5993

Website: www.parc55hotel.com

Special Rate: $125-$145

Regular Rate: $269-$289

Booking Code: USF

Cartwright Hotel on Union Square

524 Sutter Street

San Francisco, CA 94102

Reservations Line: (800) 919-9779

Direct Line: (415) 421-2865

Fax: (415) 398-6345

E-mail: reservations@cartwrighthotel.com

Website: www.cartwrighthotel.com

Special Rate: $89

Regular Rate: $129

Booking Code: USF

Financial District/ Chinatown:

Hyatt Regency San Francisco

5 Embarcadero Center

San Francisco, CA 94121

Reservation Line: (800) 233-1234

Direct Line: (415) 788-1234

Fax: (415) 981-3638

E-mail: swilliam@sforspo.hyatt.com

Website: www.hyatt.com

Special Rate: $139

Regular Rate: $285-$310

Booking Code: Please call (800) 233-1234 and ask for the USF Graduation rate.

Park Hyatt

San Francisco

333 Battery Street

San Francisco, CA 94111

Reservation Line: (415) 392-1234

Fax: (415) 296-2995

Website: www.parkhyatt.com

Special Rate: $280/$285 weekend package

Regular Rate: $315-$340

Booking Code: USF

→

Fisherman's Wharf

Hilton San Francisco Fisherman's Wharf

2620 Jones Street

San Francisco, CA 94133

Reservation Line: (415) 885-4700

Fax: (415) 351-1924

E-mail: gsmith@hiltonwharf.com

Website: www.hilton.com

Special package: $161 room + parking

Regular Rate: $149

Sheraton Fisherman's Wharf Hotel

2500 Mason Street

San Francisco, CA 94133

Reservation Line: (800) 325-3535

Direct Line: (415) 362-5500

Fax: (415) 956-5275

E-mail: Linda.dair@ilro.com

Website: www.sheratonat-thewharf.com

Special Rate: $129

Regular Rate: $229

Booking Code: USF

SF Marriott Fisherman's Wharf

1250 Columbus Avenue

San Francisco, CA 94133

Reservation Line: (800) 288-9290

Direct Line: (415) 775-5555

Fax: (415) 771-9076

Website: www.marriott.com

Special Package: $159 room + parking

Special Rate: $139

Pacific Heights

Holiday Inn Golden Gateway

1500 Van Ness Avenue

San Francisco, CA 94109

Reservation Line: (800) HOLI-DAY

Direct Line: (415) 441-4000

Fax: (415) 775-5425

E-mail: reservations@sfhigg.com

Website: http://www.holiday-inn.com/sfo-gate

Special Rate: $99-$114

Regular Rate: $139-$154

Booking Code: 100205392

Take a Campus Virtual Tour:

http://www.usfca.edu/acadserv/vrtour

To Schedule a Group Information Session or Interview:

Contact the Office of Admission by calling (800) CALL USF or (415) 422-6563. You can also fill out a request form online at http://www.usfca.edu/acadserv/admission/visit.html

Campus Tours:

A combined walking campus tour and group information session departs from the Office of Admission most weekdays (Monday-Friday) at 10 a.m. and 2 p.m. There are no tours available on Saturdays, Sundays, or Federal Holidays.

During the months of March and April, there are Information Sessions especially designed only for Accepted Students at 1 p.m. with a campus tour that follows.

Overnight Visits:

Overnight visits are only available during orientation for accepted students during the summer. Saturday visits are available on Special USF Visit Days, which are scheduled during the fall semester and begin at 10 a.m. Campus Tours, a Group Information Sessions, and Lunches are included. Contact the Admissions Office in advance.

Directions to Campus

Traveling South from the Golden Gate Bridge/North Bay

- After crossing the Golden Gate Bridge, stay in the right lane and take the 19th Avenue exit.
- Turn right on Cabrillo Street and then left onto Fourteenth Avenue.
- Proceed to Fulton Street and turn left.
- At the top of the hill, turn left onto Parker Avenue and then right onto Golden Gate Avenue.
- Proceed to the visitor's entrance on Golden Gate between Kittredge Terrace and Roselyn Terrace.

Traveling West from the Bay Bridge/East Bay

- After crossing the Bay Bridge, take the Ninth Street/Civic Center exit.
- Head westbound on Harrison Street for 1 block then turn right onto Ninth Street.
- Once on Ninth, stay in either of the two left lanes and veer onto Hayes Street.
- Continue on Hayes for eight blocks to Webster Street.
- Turn right onto Webster and proceed two blocks to Fulton Street.
- Turn left onto Fulton and continue approximately one mile to Parker Avenue (St. Ignatius Church will be on your right.)
- Turn right onto Parker and continue to Golden Gate Avenue.
- Turn right onto Golden Gate and proceed to the visitor's entrance (located to your right between Kittredge Terrace and Roselyn Terrace.)

Traveling North from the Peninsula

- Take Highway 280 Northbound.
- Take the Nineteenth Avenue exit. Stay on Nineteenth Avenue for approximately three miles.
- Turn right onto Fulton Street.
- At the top of the hill, turn left onto Parker Avenue and then right onto Golden Gate Avenue.
- Proceed to the visitor's entrance on Golden Gate between Kittredge Terrace and Roselyn Terrace.

Traveling North From San Jose/South Bay

- Take Highway 101 Northbound.
- Once in San Francisco, take the Ninth Street/Civic Center exit.
- Head westbound on Harrison Street for one block then turn right onto Ninth Street.
- Once on Ninth, stay in two left lanes and veer onto Hayes Street.
- Continue on Hayes for eight blocks to Webster Street. Turn right onto Webster and proceed two blocks to Fulton Street.
- Turn left onto Fulton and continue approximately one mile to Parker Avenue (St. Ignatius Church will be on your right.)
- Turn right onto Parker and continue to Golden Gate Avenue.
- Turn right onto Golden Gate and proceed to the visitor's entrance (located to your right between Kittredge Terrace and Roselyn Terrace.)

To reach Lone Mountain Campus, follow the above directions. Instead of turning right on Golden Gate Avenue, proceed one block north to Turk Street. Turn left onto the ramp between Parker Avenue and Temescal Street.

Words to Know

Academic Probation – A student can receive this if they fail to keep up with their school's academic minimums. Those who are unable to improve their grades after receiving this warning can possibly face dismissal.

Beer Pong / Beirut – A drinking game with numerous cups of beer arranged in a particular pattern on each side of a table. The goal is to get a ping pong ball into one of the opponent's cups by throwing the ball or hitting it with a paddle. If the ball lands in a cup, the opponent is required to drink the beer.

Bid – An invitation from a fraternity or sorority to pledge their specific house.

Blue-Light Phone – Brightly-colored phone posts with a blue light bulb on top. These phones exist for security purposes and are located at various outside locations around most campuses. If a student has an emergency or is feeling endangered, they can pick up one of these phones (free of charge) to connect with campus police or an escort service.

Campus Police – Policemen who are specifically assigned to a given institution. Campus police are not regular city officers; they are employed by the university in a full-time capacity.

Club Sports – A level of sports that falls somewhere between varsity and intramural. If a student is unable to commit to a varsity team but has a lot of passion for athletics, a club sport could be a better, less intense option. If a club sport still requires too much commitment, intramurals often involve no traveling and a lot less time.

Cocaine – An illegal drug. Also known as "coke" or "blow," cocaine often resembles a white crystalline or powdery substance. It is highly addictive and dangerous.

Common Application – An application that students can use to apply to multiple schools.

Course Registration – The time when a student selects what courses they would like for the upcoming quarter or semester. Prior to registration, it is best to have an idea of several back-up courses in case a particular class becomes full. If a course is full, a student can place themselves on the waitlist, although this still does not guarantee entry.

Division Athletics – Athletics range from Division I to Division III. Division IA is the most competitive, while Division III is considered to be the least competitive.

Dorm – Short for dormitory, a dorm is an on-campus housing facility. Dorms can provide a range of options from suite-style rooms to more communal options that include shared bathrooms. Most first-year students live in dorms. Some upper-classmen who wish to stay on campus also choose this option.

Early Action – A way to apply to a school and get an early acceptance response without a binding commitment. This is a system that is becoming less and less available.

Early Decision – An option that students should use only if they are positive that a place is their dream school. If a student applies to a school using the early decision option and is admitted, they are required and bound to attend that university. Admission rates are usually higher with early decision students because the school knows that a student is making them their first choice.

Ecstasy – An illegal drug. Also known as "E" or "X," ecstasy looks like a pill and most resembles an aspirin. Considered a party drug, ecstasy is very dangerous and can be deadly.

Ethernet – An extremely fast internet connection that is usually available in most university-owned residence halls. To use an Ethernet connection properly, a student will need a network card and cable for their computer.

Fake ID – A counterfeit identification card that contains false information. Most commonly, students get fake IDs and change their birthdates so that they appear to be older than 21 (of legal drinking age). Even though it is illegal, many college students have fake IDs in hopes of purchasing alcohol or getting into bars.

Frosh – Slang for "freshmen."

Hazing – Initiation rituals that must be completed for membership into some fraternities or sororities. Numerous universities have outlawed hazing due to its degrading or dangerous requirements.

Sports (IMs) – A popular, and usually free, student activity where students create teams and compete against other groups for fun. These sports vary in competitiveness and can include a range of activities—everything from billiards to water polo. IM sports are a great way to meet people with similar interests.

Keg – Officially called a half barrel, a keg contains roughly 200 12-ounce servings of beer and is often found at college parties.

LSD – An illegal drug. Also known as acid, this hallucinogenic drug most commonly resembles a tab of paper.

Marijuana – An illegal drug. Also known as weed or pot; besides alcohol, marijuana is one of the most commonly-found drugs on campuses across the country.

Major –The focal point of a student's college studies; a specific topic that is studied for a degree. Examples of majors include physics, English, history, computer science, economics, business, and music. Many students decide on a specific major before arriving on campus, while others are simply "undecided" and figure it out later. Those who are extremely interested in two areas can also choose to double major.

Meal Block – The equivalent of one meal. Students on a "meal plan" usually receive a fixed number of meals per week.

Each meal, or "block," can be redeemed at the school's dining facilities in place of cash. More often than not, if a student fails to use their weekly allotment of meal blocks, they will be forfeited.

Minor – An additional focal point in a student's education. Often serving as a compliment or addition to a student's main area of focus, a minor has fewer requirements and prerequisites to fulfill than a major. Minors are not required for graduation from most schools; however some students who want to further explore many different interests choose to have both a major and a minor.

Mushrooms – An illegal drug. Also known as "shrooms," this drug looks like regular mushrooms but are extremely hallucinogenic.

Off-Campus Housing – Housing from a particular landlord or rental group that is not affiliated with the university. Depending on the college, off-campus housing can range from extremely popular to non-existent. Those students who choose to live off campus are typically given more freedom, but they also have to deal with things such as possible subletting scenarios, furniture, and bills. In addition to these factors, rental prices and distance often affect a student's decision to move off campus.

Office Hours – Time that teachers set aside for students who have questions about the coursework. Office hours are a good place for students to go over any problems and to show interest in the subject material.

Pledging – The time after a student has gone through rush, received a bid, and has chosen a particular fraternity or sorority they would like to join. Pledging usually lasts anywhere from one to two semesters. Once the pledging period is complete and a particular student has done everything that is required to become a member, they are considered a brother or sister. If a fraternity or a sorority would decide to "haze" a group of students, these initiation rituals would take place during the pledging period.

Private Institution – A school that does not use taxpayers dollars to help subsidize education costs. Private schools typically cost more than public schools and are usually smaller.

Prof – Slang for "professor."

Public Institution – A school that uses taxpayers dollars to help subsidize education costs. Public schools are often a good value for in-state residents and tend to be larger than most private colleges.

Quarter System (sometimes referred to as the Trimester System) – A type of academic calendar system. In this setup, students take classes for three academic periods. The first quarter usually starts in late September or early October and concludes right before Christmas. The second quarter usually starts around early to mid–January and finishes up around March or April. The last quarter, or "third quarter," usually starts in late March or early April and finishes up in late May or Mid-June. The fourth quarter is summer. The major difference between the quarter system and semester system is that students take more courses but with less coverage.

RA (Resident Assistant) – A student leader who is assigned to a particular floor in a dormitory in order to help to the other students who live there. A RA's duties include ensuring student safety and providing guidance or assistance wherever possible.

Recitation – An extension of a specific course; a "review" session of sorts. Because some classes are so large, recitations offer a setting with fewer students where students can ask questions and get help from professors or TAs in a more personalized environment. As a result, it is common for most large lecture classes to be supplemented with recitations.

Rolling Admissions – A form of admissions. Most commonly found at public institutions, schools with this type of policy continue to accept students throughout the year until their class sizes are met. For example, some schools begin accepting students as early as December and will continue to do so until April or May.

Room and Board – This is typically the combined cost of a university-owned room and a meal plan.

Room Draw/Housing Lottery – A common way to pick on-campus room assignments for the following year. If a student decides to remain in university-owned housing, they are assigned a unique number that, along with seniority, is used to choose their new rooms for the next year.

Rush – The period in which students can meet the brothers and sisters of a particular chapter and find out if a given fraternity or sorority is right for them. Rushing a fraternity or a sorority is not a requirement at any school. The goal of rush is to give students who are serious about pledging a feel for what to expect.

Semester System – The most common type of academic calendar system at college campuses. This setup typically includes two semesters in a given school year. The "fall" semester starts around the end of August or early September and finishes right before winter vacation. The "spring" semester usually starts in mid-January and ends around late April or May.

Student Center/Rec Center/Student Union – A common area on campus that often contains study areas, recreation facilities, and eateries. This building is often a good place to meet up with fellow students and is most commonly used as a hangout. Depending on the school, the student center can have a huge role or a non-existent role in campus life.

Student ID – A university-issued photo ID that serves as a student's key to many different functions within an institution. Some schools require students to show these cards in order to get into dorms, libraries, cafeterias, and other facilities. In addition to storing meal plan information, in some cases, a student ID can actually work as a debit card and allow students to purchase things from bookstores or local shops.

Suite – A type of dorm room. Unlike other places that have communal bathrooms that are shared by the entire floor, a suite has a private bathroom. Suite-style dorm rooms can house anywhere from two to ten students.

TA (Teacher's Assistant) – An undergraduate or grad student who helps in some manner with a specific course. In some cases, a TA will teach a class, assist a professor, grade assignments, or conduct office hours.

Undergraduate – A student who is in the process of studying for their Bachelor (college) degree.

ABOUT THE AUTHOR:

I feel like I should open this section with the standard "Sara Allshouse is the author of many short stories and currently lives in San Francisco with her two cats". But I will tell you something more interesting instead, like that I write fiction for fun; I am about to graduate from USF with an English writing major and a politics minor and then go to law school. I watch Sex and the City and The West Wing religiously, and if it weren't for those shows, I wouldn't have made it through college. More importantly, I want to say I've had the best time writing this book-not only because I'll be published (though the prospect is not too shabby), but also because this opportunity, especially coming at the end of my undergraduate career, feels like a hands-on culmination of everything I've ever learned. Honestly, I've never worked so hard or so long on one thing, so seeing the results of my efforts will be absolutely exhilarating!

So please, read and re-read this book and memorize all of the facts because you're lucky to have them available to you in one place. College Prowler really does provide an insider look that is much more helpful than any book I ever read before going to college. Enjoy, and I do hope you choose USF, because it really does rock!

Sara Allshouse

SaraAllshouse@collegeprowler.com

Notes

....

....

....

....

....

....

....

....

....

....

....

....

....

Notes

....

....

....

....

....

....

....

....

....

....

....

....

....

Notes

Notes

....

....

....

....

....

....

....

....

....

....

....

....

....

Notes

....

....

....

....

....

....

....

....

....

....

....

....

Notes

....

....

....

....

....

....

....

....

....

....

....

....

....

Notes

....

....

....

....

....

....

....

....

....

....

....

....

....

Notes

....

....

....

....

....

....

....

....

....

....

....

....

....

Notes

....

....

....

....

....

....

....

....

....

....

....

....

....

Notes

....

....

....

....

....

....

....

....

....

....

....

....

....

Notes

....

....

....

....

....

....

....

....

....

....

....

....

....

Notes

....

....

....

....

....

....

....

....

....

....

....

....

....

Notes

....

....

....

....

....

....

....

....

....

....

....

....

....

Notes

....

....

....

....

....

....

....

....

....

....

....

....

....

Notes

....

....

....

....

....

....

....

....

....

....

....

....

....

Notes

....

....

....

....

....

....

....

....

....

....

....

....

....

....

Notes

....

....

....

....

....

....

....

....

....

....

....

....

....

Notes

....

....

....

....

....

....

....

....

....

....

....

....

....

Need More Help?

Do you have more questions about this school? Can't find a certain statistic? College Prowler is here to help. We are the best source of college information on the planet. We have a network of thousands of students who can get the latest information on any school to you ASAP. E-mail us at *info@collegeprowler.com* with your college-related questions. It's like having an older sibling show you the ropes!

Email Us Your College-Related Questions!

Check out **www.collegeprowler.com** for more details.
1.800.290.2682

Notes

....

....

....

....

....

....

....

....

....

....

....

....

....

Tell Us What Life Is Really Like At Your School!

Have you ever wanted to let people know what your school is really like? Now's your chance to help millions of high school students choose the right school.

Let your voice be heard and win cash and prizes!

Check out **www.collegeprowler.com** for more info!

Notes

....

....

....

....

....

....

....

....

....

....

....

....

....

Do You Have What It Takes To Get Admitted?

The College Prowler Road to College Counseling Program is here. An admissions officer will review your candidacy at the school of your choice and create a 12+ page personal admission plan. We rate your credentials with the same criteria used by school admissions committees. We assess your strengths and weaknesses and create a plan of action that makes a difference.

Check out **www.collegeprowler.com** or call 1.800.290.2682 for complete details.

Notes

....

....

....

....

....

....

....

....

....

....

....

....

....

....

Pros and Cons

Still can't figure out if this is the right school for you?
You've already read through this in-depth guide; why not
list the pros and cons? It will really help with narrowing down
your decision and determining whether or not
this school is right for you.

Pros	Cons

Notes

....

....

....

....

....

....

....

....

....

....

....

....

....

Notes

....

....

....

....

....

....

....

....

....

....

....

....

....

Get Paid To Rep Your City!

Make money for college!

Earn cash by telling your friends about College Prowler!

Excellent Pay + Incentives + Bonuses

Compete with reps across the nation for cash bonuses

Gain marketing and communication skills

Build your resume and gain work experience for future career opportunities

Flexible work hours; make your own schedule

Opportunities for advancement

Contact *sales@collegeprowler.com*
Apply now at **www.collegeprowler.com**

Notes

....

....

....

....

....

....

....

....

....

....

....

....

....

Notes

....

....

....

....

....

....

....

....

....

....

....

....

....

Reach A Market Of Over 24 Million People.

Advertising with College Prowler will provide you with an environment in which your message will be read and respected. Place your message in a College Prowler guidebook, and let us start bringing long-lasting customers to you. We deliver high-quality ads in color or black-and-white throughout our guidebooks.

Contact Joey Rahimi
joey@collegeprowler.com
412.697.1391
1.800.290.2682

Check out **www.collegeprowler.com** for more info.

Notes

....
....
....
....
....
....
....
....
....
....
....
....
....

Write For Us!

Get Published! Voice Your Opinion.

Writing a College Prowler guidebook is both fun and rewarding; our open-ended format allows your own creativity free reign. Our writers have been featured in national newspapers and have seen their names in bookstores across the country. Now is your chance to break into the publishing industry with one of the country's fastest-growing publishers!

Apply now at **www.collegeprowler.com**

Contact *editor@collegeprowler.com* or call 1.800.290.2682 for more details.